Hello Mary Kay!

Enjoy my love

letter to the South

of France!

François

Cuisine of the Sun

A Ray of Sunshine on Your Plate

Cuisine of the Sun
A Ray of Sunshine on Your Plate

Written and Photographed by François de Mélogue

ISBN 978-0-692-53747-3

Printed by Worzalla

Manufactured in the United States

Cover design by Lemon Fresh Design

Interior design by Lemon Fresh Design

Edited by Lisa de Mélogue

Distributed by Eat Till You Bleed
www.EatTillYouBleed.com

A very special thanks must go out to eight people whose extraordinary generosity enabled this dream to become a reality:

Michael Vaughn

Christopher Lye

Walter Kinney

Scott Glassman

Myrna Lo

Jack & Peggy Ridley

David Young

Table of Contents

"Cooking is like love. It should be entered into with abandon or not at all. This, then, is not a document for jiffy cooks. Nor for those devotees of those premixed, prewhipped, pre-stewed foods that crowd the grocer's shelf."
- Harriet Van Horne

Giving Thanks

Where do I begin to thank all the people that I owe extreme debts of gratitude to, yet could never begin to repay? First and foremost this book is dedicated to my perfect, beautiful little son Beaumont. If he were reading this as his four year old self he would correct me and say his name was Beau, not Beaumont. Beaumont is only what I call him when I am angry. I understand what life is about because of you, Beau. Massive thanks go to my wife Lisa who had to put up with my irrational temper tantrums while trying to write this book. To borrow an overused line, you make me complete. She hates when I say that, but it is true. Without her I would be lost. I have become a closet alcoholic trying to write this book. Lisa will be flipping the bill for detox when it is all done. I have to thank my beautiful maman Micheline (whom I lovingly called Mishou all my life), for without her this book could never be. She is the most amazing mother any child could ever hope or dream for. To Dr. Karl Fritz, who believed in me way before anyone else did. He fostered and inspired my foray into photography, though please do not blame him for my questionable works. Huge thanks to Joan and Gary Verne for being the absolute best in-laws ever. The well of their love and support is truly bottomless. Without their unceasing help, none of this could have ever happened. I thank my grandfather Andre Colas for teaching me to love foie gras, truffles, Chateau Margaux and even my own pet rabbits. Thanks for cooking them when I was seven. It is the exact moment I knew I would become a Chef. Above all, I want to thank my father. Even in death, I can feel his hand guide mine when I doubt myself, and God knows that is often.

I have to thank the countless people that have inspired my career and pushed me to be better. Many I have never personally met or even lived in the same century with. Some I was fortunate to have been in their presence, even if only shortly. I thank Michel LeBorgne, Franklin Biggs, Louis Szathmary—these three were my early mentors that will forever hold a very special place in my heart. I feel the need to thank the Chefs throughout history who carried the torch known as *le feu sacre*, or the sacred fire, from one kitchen to the next throughout countless centuries. It is the true unwritten, oral history of food through time immortal that passed through kitchens, both professional and at home. I thank Careme, Urbain DuBois, Escoffier, Fernand Point, Mere Brazier, Alain Chapel, Paul Bocuse, Joel Robuchon, Alain Ducasse, Jacques Pepin (God, I love Jacques), Julia Child, Paula Wolfert, Colman Andrews, Waverly Root, Paul Bertolli. Really, this list is as vast as the stars that light the night sky.

I need to thank the countless people with whom I had the good fortune to work. All of you made me a better cook and a better person. A few truly stand out. I want to personally thank Beau MacMillan who started his culinary life as my kitchen bitch. He is an ego-less giant standing tall among men; Dave Mottershall, who could crush it like no other, Doug Eisler and Jason Stefanikis, who joined me on so many crazy adventures in so many different kitchens. To my brother Peter Zitz, whom I love as much as I do Provence. And Alex Hernandez and Keith, who stood next to me in the final days.

This book is dedicated to every single person that supported my dreams. I realize now in my drunken stupor I probably left off some key people. Completely unintentional and not meant. My life is forever enriched by your presence.
~ François

1

Le Feu Sacre, The Story of Me

This book is the culmination of a lifetime spent relentlessly dreaming of food while toiling away in hot kitchens, both professional and at home. My life story is that of a son of an immigrant mother whose French culture and joie de vivre founded and shaped the foodie and person I am today.

Food shaped my story from the very beginning. While I was in the womb my grandfather Pépé insisted on feeding my pregnant mother a hearty Perigord diet of goose foie gras and black truffles to ensure that, despite growing up in the savage New World thousands of miles from the French motherland, I would become a proper gourmet. The feasting continued on day one when, instead of getting the traditional spank and sip of mother's milk to herald my arrival, I was handed a flute of bubbles and a serious addiction to the good life. You see, dear old Maman was born in Champagne, France and it is the age-old custom to wet the lips of a newborn with a sparkler. The way she recounts my birth is: I was being ingloriously hung upside down like a rabbit about to be spanked when she growled at the doctor with a devil-like ferocity that I needed a flute of Champagne immediately. It's best not to question a command emitted forcibly from a snarling woman who just had the equivalent of a melon pass through the most intimate part of her anatomy and survive to tell the tale.

I grew up in Chicago, living life on the fence between two cultures, French and American. I should throw in a third because of the strong influence of Zenita Shaw, our childhood Nanny who looked after me and my sister so both parents could work. Zenita was an amazing African American woman with deep Southern roots and a heart of pure gold. Widespread violence broke out in Chicago the day Martin Luther King was assassinated. Zenita took me into her home and kept me safe on the south side hidden in plain view. Chickens were frying and pots of collards stewing amidst the crackle of gunfire resonating in the streets. It was my first direct exposure to Southern food and culture and it profoundly affected my palate.

My parents met at the University of Chicago, where all the Europeans naturally gathered together to share in familiar cultural experiences. The Raineri's were an Italian family who lived below us and shared many Sunday meals together. Vittorio, the patriarch of the family, was a typical Italian who insisted on authentic Italian flavors and great espresso. So much so that he drove 90 miles one way to Wisconsin to get fresh spring water for his coffee. We often accompanied him on shopping forays to Chicago's Taylor Street where we shopped for groceries amid Chicago's Little Italy. Vittorio found enough imported pastas, prosciutto, San Marzano tomatoes, cheeses, spices and other food stuffs to make these Sunday meals feel like vacations to Tuscany.

My mother came from a wealthy family that lived in the south of France. The extent of her food education prior to meeting my father was learned eating in restaurants like L'Oustau de Baumaniere in Provence, Pieds de Cochon in Paris or having her father's cook Mémé prepare dinner. Ironically, my mother herself learned to cook by reading Julia Child's seminal book 'Mastering the Art of French Cooking'. Through Julia, she was reunited with her mother culture and proudly fed us a different meal every single night (my father's requirement). My first moments in the kitchen were spent hanging on my mother's apron strings pretending to be a more French version of Julia.

No feat was too daunting or act unworthy of ultimate sacrifice to ensure a proper meal with the correct ambiance at her table. One of the great stories of my childhood was of a Moroccan party my mother threw for the European expats. My mother had sawed off all the legs of our dining room table and ringed it with all of our household cushions to provide the proper mood for a lavish Moroccan feast. I will never forget the mixed look of horror and anger on my father's face as he arrived home that night. As much as my mother's free spiritedness and love of life caused my father to utter 'mon dieu' all too often, I knew he secretly loved it. Shortly after he passed I came across a letter from 1958 in which he glowed about my mother's magic to a dear friend. He had kept all those years in a special box.

The pets of our household didn't fare too well in my early years. I filleted my sister's goldfish at age two and braised my pet rabbits by age seven. My mother worked as a nurse, running the ENT department at Billings Hospital. One day she came home with a live turkey given to a parting doctor as a gag gift. The turkey ran around our condominium's basement hallways till the neighbors complained and she worked up the courage to send old Tom on his way to the next incarnation. Holding the turkey neck in one hand and wielding a Chinese cleaver with all her might, she muttered a prayer and swung with eyes closed, severing the top of her finger off. Before going to the hospital she punted the turkey out into the streets. It was last seen crossing the Midway Plaisance towards the ghetto to undoubtedly face a fate equally perilous to the one it just had escaped.

My early years in the kitchen didn't always fare too well for my father either. I can still remember the day my mother was replacing all of her spices. She had given them to me to play with. I gathered them together and made a brick reddish 'stew' of cayenne pepper, cinnamon, paprika, mace and everything else my mother had discarded. My father came home and walked into the kitchen. He saw a tomato sauce simmering on the stovetop and naturally assumed I was playing with a small variation of it on the floor. He took a big spoonful and almost choked to death on the intense heat. The lesson seared into my brain, resurrected now that I am teaching my own four year old son how to cook: Never taste anything blindly.

It may be cliché to claim one learned to cook hanging off their maman's apron strings, but I really did. She was a free spirited natural who cooked like a jazz musician riffs. Edible poetry in constant motion. She had a fearless style that was never daunted by lengthy recipes or even the need to follow them religiously. On the spot substitutions when ingredients could not be found were the norm. New innovations were created nightly. Her food was imbued with a generous helping of love and passion, and it is that style that I learned. I often told apprentices in my kitchens that you can give two equal cooks the exact same bag of groceries and even the same recipe and you will end up with two different dishes. The person who cooks with passion and love always prepares the tastier, more soul satisfying meal. Think of a French or Italian grandmother hovering over a pot of something simmering. Surely they are approaching cooking without worrying about the Maillard reaction. Cooking and eating is so much more an emotional act than one of science. Sure, it would be foolish to say science does not apply. When we discuss science versus passion we talk about what approach the cook takes. Marcus Samuelsson once said "You have to balance, but you can be aggressive as a Chef. It benefits the food. You have to be passionate. You can't be angry cooking." Emotion is intoned and verbalized in food. Food and emotion are so strongly interconnected perhaps science cannot rationally document that phenomena.

I followed the natural path from budding gourmet to becoming a Chef, cutting my teeth on a cornucopia of restaurants across the USA, Canada and even a brief stage for Joel Robuchon in Paris. I am honored to have graduated from one of the first classes of the New England Culinary Institute and developed my chops under such great mentors as Michel LeBorgne, Michel Martinez, Danny Michaud, and David Miles.

I will never forget the day Chef Louis Szathmary came to talk to us at school. His electrified speech sent shivers down my spine and crystallized my need to be in a professional kitchen. Chef Louis was a character straight out of the classic European kitchens of yesteryear about which I fantasized. He told me he began his cooking career as an OSS agent stationed at the Hotel Adlon during World War II in Berlin. Over the course of his lengthy career he accomplished so much it would be

impossible to mention everything. What struck me most was developing food for the space program, creating Stouffer's first five frozen dishes (including the spinach soufflé I ate a lot of in the 1960's) and most importantly, he initiated the change in status of Chefs in America. Prior to 1974, cooks were listed as domestics according to the Federal government. This may seem like a minor event in our current world of celebrity Chefs, but it was a major point back then. He realized this when he tried to get credit at Marshall Fields. He was asked his career and then told he was not qualified for credit as a domestic. He began the push that elevated Chefs and cooking into a respected profession. I had the great fortune to start first as a commis and then return as his Executive Chef. I fondly remember Louis and wish he were still here.

Life in kitchens was far from serious. To break the monotony of lengthy hours and sweating in hot kitchens, we played a lot of practical jokes. The hard work spawned a sense of humor bordering on the perverse. Louis' kitchen was staffed with an oddball collection of Eastern Europeans. Two stories jump out in my mind. We had a young artist named Miklos whose father came to visit for a brief period. Sandor was the senior executive chef for the communist party in Hungary dating way back. Despite his advanced age, Sandor was built like a tank and worked harder than anyone else. We held a party in his honor inviting many Chicago area socialites. Sandor barely spoke English and would just smile, nod and say thank you to everyone. I pulled him aside with a feigned look of horror and told him through choreographed pantomimes that what he was saying was completely wrong and even terrible. In mock horror I pantomimed what Sandor was saying. He looked absolutely horrified then thanked me and walked back into the dining room bowing to all the socialites proudly exclaiming "fuck you, fuck you very much" to everyone that said anything to him.

Teodor was a Romanian porter who spotlessly cleaned the entire restaurant and apartments above with a vacuum cleaner mounted on his back and a small knife to scratch out any errant piece of gum or filth built in. Despite his smallish frame, Teodor was solid muscle. I could never really speak to him with words directly. We communicated through profane gestures and shared laughs. One night after receiving his paycheck, he went out looking for a little action. He spotted an attractive hooker walking down the street. After motioning his intentions and budget, an agreement was reached and the two started walking towards his studio apartment. What Teodor didn't realize was the "prostitute" was really an undercover cop and two Dick Butkus sized Chicago cops were monitoring him from an unmarked car. After the female cop made the sign, the two cops walked up to arrest him. Teodor thought they were trying to steal his date and in a whirlwind knocked both of them out. He started dragging the terrified female officer upstairs. Luckily Louis was very well connected and managed to get Teodor off with minor bribes. Louis was always saving people from themselves. He had a heart of gold.

I had the great pleasure to work with some truly colorful cooks and oddball characters. If I spent the rest of my life writing endlessly I could never document all the absurdities I have witnessed. Such was life in the kitchens. Anthony Bourdain's 'Kitchen Confidential' delves into a lot of what goes on so no more is really needed. Anthony and I shared two sets of bosses, though at different times, including the infamous Silver Shadow to which Tony dedicates an entire chapter.

In 2014, I left the professional ranges and moved to the Portland area to spend time with my family. My greatest pleasures now are rediscovering food through the eyes of my four year old son, Beau, who has proclaimed himself the family saucier. He has helped me rediscover my passion for food and the table, and its importance in the daily motions of life. Admittedly, I miss for the controlled chaos of restaurant service and the friendships forged in the sacred fires.

"To prepare dinner for a friend is to put into the cooking pot all one's affection and good will, all one's gaiety and zest, so that after three hours' cooking a waft of happiness escapes beneath the lid."
— Edouard de Pomiane

Some final notes before you plunge in

Every recipe is written for four people unless noted. This book is written to that young boy or girl who learns, much like myself, hanging by his mother's apron strings and watching the magic happen. This book is NOT intended for people who NEED a written recipe that is completely bulletproof and dumbed down—over simplified recipes that no longer resemble the original.

Assume every recipe calls for seasoning with sea salt, even if I left it out. I only use unsalted butter in my recipes. Salted butter is saved for eating raw radishes. Do not try to make my pistou recipe listed here in the wintertime, it won't work. Instead, follow the spirit of the dish and use winter friendly ingredients. You will be amazed at how much better it will taste. Recipes are nothing more than guidelines to follow. Be liberated by that statement.

As Gustav said in the animated Disney classic 'Ratatouille', "Anyone can cook". It is so true, anyone CAN cook. All that is required is the belief and the willingness to get over the fear. It's ok to lose sight of the shores and venture fearless in search of new lands. I learned by watching my mother cook then trying, and failing, many times. It's not how many times you fall in life that count, but how many times you stand back up. I learned from my mother that sometimes what seems to be a failure is really a new and exciting dish.

I believe it was the late, great French Chef Escoffier who once said that we as cooks can never hope to surpass the quality of ingredients we start with. To make a great meal out of mediocre ingredients is impossible. If you ask me about the state of food in America I am both a pessimist and an optimist. When I shop at most grocery stores I am amazed at the lack of regionality and diversity. Most ingredients have traveled far and lost most of their flavor in the process, perhaps even stopping at a chemical plant along the way for unhealthy additions. If I look at my simple farmer's market in Portland, Oregon then I am hopeful beyond belief. The breadth of choices is astonishing and the offerings change almost weekly. Ma and pa food artisans have taken their rightful place next to small scale farmers, ranchers and fishermen. It gives me hope that once again food is being respected and loved in this country. I ask you, no I beg you, to be very selective in your ingredient choices. There is a perceptible difference in the quality of ingredients. Grass-fed meats and their dairy products taste better than the commodity meats and dairy products. Wild fish simply is better than farmed in every circumstance. It's ok, call me a food snob.

Do not be lazy. Good food takes time. Put your smartphone down, turn off the TV and enjoy your family. Involve your children in food. Show them what an apple orchard looks like or a farm. Teach them the relationships between the earth, the plow, the table and your stomach. Enjoy!

Some of my favorite specialty ingredients and recommended kitchen tools can be found in the Resources section of my blog, www.EatTillYouBleed.com

Tapenade
Black Olive Puree with Capers and Anchovies

When the weather starts to heat up, my tastes venture to the South of France, long renowned for it's soul satisfying Summer food. A cuisine rich with condiments like rouille and tapenado that just seem to enhance everything. The word tapenade is derived from the Provençal word for capers, tapeno. Early tapenade recipes included fresh tuna although most these days use anchovy. I love eating tapenade on everything, artichokes, grilled fish, roast chicken and even smeared on tartines with fresh goat cheese. . . . .

Quintessential Tapenado
2 cups pitted Kalamata olives
4 tablespoons capers
1 small tin anchovies
8 basil leaves
1/4 cup fragrant French olive oil

Green Tapenado with Preserved Tuna Belly and Lemon
2 cups pitted Picholine olives
4 tablespoons capers
1 small tin tuna belly
1/2 lemon, zested
8 basil leaves
1/4 cup fragrant French olive oil

a recipe close to the original tapenade invented by the chef of the Maison Doree in Marseille
2 cups pitted olives
4 tablespoons capers
1 ounce tin tuna belly
8 anchovy filets
1 tablespoon Dijon mustard
1/2 lemon, zested
8 basil leaves
1/4 cup fragrant French olive oil
1 teaspoon Cognac or Marc

Whichever Tapenado you make
Drain your olives well. Put everything in your food processor and pulse to the texture you like. Yes, it is as simple as that. Tapenade has a long shelf life despite the fact my tapenade never lasts more than a meal or two.

Olives
After spending a life in the kitchen I found one simple truth. Pitted olives just do not taste the same. Resist your first inclination to be lazy and buy pitted olives. They are inferior in quality and pitting olives is quick and easy. Also stand clear of canned black olives you find in American grocery stores. I am not even sure how they can ruin olives so easily but they do.

"I drink too much. The last time I gave a urine sample it had an olive in it."
-Rodney Dangerfield (1921-2004)

Warm Olives

Thyme, Orange and Garlic Confit

I cannot think of a better way to whet my appetite than to nibble on some olives and saucisson with a glass of wine. I started life as an olive purist demanding they were served simply brined and nothing else. Then I tried these. The marriage of flavors combined with the warmed aromatics make these olives irresistible. The flavors will literally jump out and seduce your palate. Change the herb combinations to suit your palate. . . . .

Garlic Confit

1/2 cup extra virgin olive oil
1 sprig fresh thyme
1 dried hot pepper
1 bay leaf
1 head of garlic, peeled

Olives

1 cup Picholine olives
1 cup Niçoise olives
1/4 teaspoon ground fennel seeds
1/2 orange, zested
1/2 teaspoon red wine vinegar

Garlic Confit

Put olive oil, thyme, hot pepper, bay leaf and garlic into a small sauce pot and bring to a boil. Reduce to a simmer and slowly cook garlic till very soft and tender, about 30 minutes. Let garlic infuse in the oil overnight.

Olives

Pour two tablespoons of the infused garlic oil in a saute pan and heat with olives, fennel, orange zest and vinegar. The idea is just to warm the olives and release the fragrant flavors of fennel and orange.

"The joy of living, I say, was summed up for me in the remembered sensation of that burning and aromatic swallow, that mixture of milk and coffee and bread by which men hold communion with tranquil pastures, exotic plantations, and golden harvests, communion with earth."
~ Antoine de Saint Exupéry

Artichoke Tarte Tatin
Carmelized Fennel and Onion, Goat Cheese, Olive Emulsion

Growing up I learned to cook at my mother's apron strings. She made a lot of tarte tatins over the course of my childhood. When I became Chef of a Southern French restaurant in Chicago I decided to honor her Provençal roots with a savory interpretation using the classic flavors of artichokes, fennel, goat cheese and olives. It became a signature dish that followed me throughout my career. . . . .

Vegetables
½ red pepper, sliced
½ fennel bulb, sliced
½ sweet onion, sliced
1 tablespoon olive oil
sea salt and black pepper

Artichokes
4 large artichokes, peeled
2 tablespoons olive oil
1 lemon, sliced

Olive emulsion
10 pitted Niçoise olives, chopped
2 egg yolks
½ teaspoon black pepper
1 teaspoon red wine vinegar
1 tablespoon mild olive oil
1 tablespoon butter, room temp

Assemble the tart
2 tablespoons olive oil
2 tablespoons shaved Parmesan
2 ounces fresh goat cheese
4 puff pastry circles

Vegetables
Sauté the vegetables in olive oil till soft and lightly caramelized. Season with sea salt and pepper, then reserve.

Artichokes
Trim artichokes using a serrated paring knife till all the outer leaves are removed and there are no more bitter dark green spots. Cut the top off just above the bottom and use a teaspoon to scoop out the choke.

Cook in rapidly boiling salted water with olive oil and sliced lemon till a paring knife easily pierces the bottoms, about ten minutes.

Olive emulsion
Mix chopped olives with egg yolks, black pepper and vinegar. Whisk over boiling water till light and creamy. Combine olive oil and butter then slowly whisk into eggs. (Same method as making a Hollandaise.)

Assemble the tart
Drizzle a little olive oil in four small blini pans. Slice artichokes thinly and fan out in the pans. Top with a generous tablespoon of the caramelized vegetables, shaved Parmesan, ½ an ounce of goat cheese then press a circle of puff pastry. The puff pastry should be a slightly larger diameter than the pan you are using. Push the edges firmly around the artichoke. Bake at 450 degrees till golden brown, about 15 to 20 minutes. Flip out onto a warmed plate, top with a spoonful of olive emulsion and enjoy!

Pistou

Vegetable, Bean and Pasta Soup

No other soup, save for bouillabaisse which really isn't a soup, clearly defines Provence more aptly than Pistou. It's the edible history of the 'arrière-pays', or hinterlands of Provence where farmers have long tended their fields of vegetables and fruits. There are several versions of Pistou ranging from ham and bean to purely vegetable. This one is based on what my maman taught me, though she would roll her eyes at the very thought of canned beans and San Marzano tomatoes—I find them to be suitable substitutes with little loss of quality or flavor. But never use store bought pesto, it will ruin the final outcome. . . . .

Serves 8

Soupe au pistou
1/4 cup olive oil
1 onion, chopped
4 carrots, chopped
1 leek, chopped, washed
4 cloves garlic, mashed
2 zucchini, chopped
1/2 can San Marzano tomatoes
2 quarts water
1 can Great Northern beans
1 cup green beans, chopped
2 potatoes, peeled and cubed
1 bay leaf
sea salt
black pepper
1 cup vermicelli, cooked
1 cup grated Gruyère or Parmesan

Pistou
3 cloves garlic, peeled
1 cup shredded Parmesan
1 fingerling potato, peeled, boiled
1 cup olive oil
4 ounces fresh basil

Soupe au pistou
Heat olive oil in a large sauce pot and lightly cook chopped onion, carrots and washed leeks. Add garlic and zucchini and continue cooking till the vegetables are softening and your kitchen is filled with a beautiful scent that would make Marcel Pagnol smile. Add tomatoes, water, beans, green beans, potatoes and bay leaf and simmer tenderly till everything is cooked, about thirty minutes. Season with sea salt and black pepper. I recommend letting soup sit overnight to develop the flavors.

Pistou
Put peeled garlic, shredded Parmesan, boiled potato and olive oil into a food processor. Puree until completely smooth.

Bring four quarts of water to a rapid boil and drop basil leaves in. Use a strainer to remove basil leaves immediately and cool off in ice water. Squeeze water out and add to pureed mixture. Process till smooth and vibrant green.

To serve, bring soup to a boil and add the cooked vermicelli. Ladle soup into bowls and garnish with a dollop of pistou and a generous pinch of grated cheese.

Burnt Fingers

Fried Calamari, Smelts, Shrimp and Vegetables, Rouille

I love whimsical menu names and thankfully Provence is full of them. Sometimes the stories intrigue me as much as the food. Fifteen years ago I read 'Feasts of Provence' by Robert Courier for the first time. The beautiful photography and carefully researched recipes transported me to Provence. A good book should do that for you. It should take you somewhere. Robert described a popular fried seafood dish served by Chef Franck Cerutti at his simple restaurant Don Camillo in Nice. The dish was called brûle doigts, or burnt fingers in English. The name implies the fish is served so hot you literally burn your fingers eating it. Now Franck is the enormously talented Chef hired by the legendary Alain Ducasse to run the kitchens at Louis XV in Monte Carlo. A must-eat spot for any serious foodie! . . . .

Marinate the Fish

8 ounces calamari, cleaned
12 - 16 smelts or small whole fish
8 shrimp, peeled and deveined
1 cup buttermilk

Prepping the Vegetables

12 slices Japanese eggplant
4 asparagus spears, cooked
12 slices zucchini

When you are ready to eat

2 cups all purpose flour
1 tablespoon herbes de Provence
2 teaspoons piment d'ville
2 teaspoons sea salt
1 recipe tempura batter
10 cups vegetable oil
2 lemons, cut into 12 wedges
1 cup rouille, see page 39

Chef's Note: There are many excellent choices available. Use your favorite store-bought tempura batter brand and make according to the directions on the box.

Marinate the Fish

Cut calamari into 1/4 inch rings. Marinate smelts, calamari and shrimp in buttermilk overnight. This tenderizes the calamari.

Prepping the Vegetables

Soak Japanese eggplant slices in ice cold water for ten minutes to remove bitterness. Drain completely then mix with asparagus and zucchini.

When you are ready to eat

Mix flour with herbes de Provence, piment d'ville and sea salt. Prepare tempura batter.

Make a batch of rouille sauce. Pour a glass of Rosé.

Heat vegetable oil to 350 degrees in a large stock pot or household fryer. Strain seafood and dredge in seasoned flour. Deep fry until golden brown and fully cooked, about five minutes. Dip vegetables in tempura batter and fry till brown and crispy, about five minutes. Drain on paper towels. Serve immediately with lemon wedges and a ramekin of rouille to dip everything in.

Visiting Boonville for its "third spice"

One of my favorite regions in America is Northern California. In a lot of ways, the picturesque Anderson Valley of Mendocino County reminds me in spirit of the South of France and Italy, though perhaps in an obscure kind of way. The sun-kissed rocky hills and foggy valley floor are home to thousands of acres of grape vines, small organic farms and herds of goats and sheep. Its bucolic small towns nestled among towering redwoods and craggy coastlines bathed in the golden California sunshine are a photographer's wet dream. Like Peter Mayle's biographical series 'A Year in Provence', Mendocino boasts a unique rhythm governed by its own cast of colorful characters that people the region. Artists, musicians, farmers, brewers, and vintners shape and enrich the colorful tapestry woven from a strong sustainable, organic and independent fabric. Time is measured not by days, weeks or months but by the seasons.

If Boonville is the cultural center of Anderson Valley life, then the Boonville Hotel has to be the incubator where ideas are contrived. I recently spoke with Kendra McEwen about piment d'ville, a fresher, more robust alternative to piment d'espelette for chefs and home cooks in America.

"Piment d'ville all started in the kitchen at the Boonville Hotel where Chef Johnny Schmitt had been using piment d'espelette for decades after he discovered it traveling around Southern France. One day he realized that we may live in the perfect climate to attempt growing the chile ourselves.

In 2010 we cultivated a pepper field out back and grew 50 plants just to see if we could do it. We were pleasantly surprised to see that our fresh product was even better than what we had been buying out of France. We renamed our variety piment d'ville in respect of the espelette AOC, and in 2011 we grew 100 plants, then 1000 plants in 2012, 5000 plants in 2013, 10,000 plants in 2014 and this year we will plant 30,000.

We grow it because we want to eat it on everything. That's the real reason. And beyond that, we want to share it with everyone and help all kitchens be equipped with this "third spice" that becomes as invaluable as salt once you've tried it. The history of our company is still being written, really, as we're only in our third year of selling commercially. We are a small town crew of spunky farmers and chefs. We do everything by hand, and we make sure to play just as hard as we work."

Moved by her story I anxiously opened the tin. Immediately I noticed how much fresher it was than its French counterpart. I was blown away by the vitality of complex flavors of smoky sweet peppers punctuated with hints of tobacco. The vibrant red brick ground peppers had a beautiful mild and lingering heat that would complement food well. Piment d'ville is what I imagine tasting espelettes at the source must be like. I went home that night and eagerly compared the two. My espelette peppers were more of an orangish color with subdued flavors and a slight staleness. I preferred the piment d'ville which Kendra lovingly calls the third spice. I told her it's so good it should be the first.

www.pimentdville.com

Grilled Sardines

Fresh Herbes de Provence, Salted Capers and Charred Lemon

Sardines are a full flavored fish that people will either love or love to hate. They have an incredible oily texture and intense pungent flavor that lends itself to grilling or sautéing. I prefer them grilled over charcoal with the fire licking the edges, leaving them slightly blackened and crispy. I serve them in a rich, buttery sauce full of sharp contrasting flavors. Explosions of lemon, capers and hot peppers burst in every bite. . . . .

Marinate

2 pounds sardines
1 cup extra virgin olive oil
1 lemon, zested, save juice for sauce
3 tablespoons chopped savory, marjoram, rosemary, thyme and
    oregano

Sauce and Cooking

3 tablespoons butter
2 tablespoons garlic, rough chopped
1 teaspoon chili flakes
3 tablespoons salted capers
3 tablespoons chopped savory, marjoram, rosemary, thyme and
    oregano

To Finish

to taste, sea salt and piment d'ville
3 lemons, cut in ½, charred

Chef's Note: This recipe uses fresh versions of the same herbs found in herbes de Provence. Traditionally, lavender was never put in herbes de Provence. That was something added for the American market who associate Provence with the beautiful lavender fields.

Marinate

Marinate fresh sardines in olive oil, lemon zest and herbs for a few hours, or overnight.

Sauce and Cooking

Build a big fire in your grill using wood charcoal. Charcoal grills are always preferable to gas grills for a lot of reasons, the main one is that wonderful smoky flavor.

Prepare the sauce while your coals are getting hot. Melt one tablespoon of butter and sauté garlic and chili flakes till garlic turns a light amber color. Add salted capers, fresh herbs and lemon juice. Whisk in remaining two tablespoons of butter. Keep sauce warm.

To Finish

Season sardines with sea salt and piment d'ville then cook over a hot, fiery coal bed. You want flames to rise up and burn the edges of the fish turning them into crispy charred bits.

Arrange on a big platter and pour sauce over. Surround the fish with charred lemon and enjoy with a chilled Rosé!

I absolutely adore charred lemons. It imparts an irresistibly sweet and smoky quality. I make them one of two ways, on a grill or in a really hot saute pan. Cut the lemon in half and cook cut side down till blackened.

Tuna Niçoise Crudo

Eggs, Green Beans, Fingerling Potatoes, Olives and Tomatoes

A fun, contemporary twist on the eternal Salade Niçoise. Here tuna appears as a crudo, taking the center stage. It provides a savory canvas for fresh vegetables to play off of. Substitute any sushi grade fish in its place. This salad works with everything from raw scallops to hamachi. . . . .

Prepare the Vegetables
12 cherry tomato confit, page 73
16 green beans, blanched
1/2 red onion, sliced thin
2 piquillo peppers, julienned
12 fingerling potatoes, boil, halve
1/4 cup niçoise olives
1/2 lemon, squeezed
3 tablespoons fruity extra virgin olive oil
4 leaves of basil, cut thinly
sea salt and black pepper

Finishing the Salad
12 ounces sushi grade tuna
fruity extra virgin olive oil
sea salt and black pepper
2 hard boiled eggs,
peeled and cut into quarters

Prepare the Vegetables
Combine tomato confit, green beans, red onions, piquillo peppers, fingerling potatoes and Niçoise olives. Toss with lemon juice, olive oil and basil. Season with sea salt and black pepper.

I do not like refrigerating the vegetables for this salad as it changes the textures too much. Boiled potatoes become denser and less creamy, red onions loses their crunch and cold tomatoes don't have the same flavor impact. It is better to prepare this a few hours ahead and leave in a cool place in your kitchen.

Finishing the Salad
Cut the tuna into super thin slices and divide among four chilled plates. Drizzle a touch of olive oil and season with sea salt and black pepper. Artistically arrange the salad on top of the tuna. Decorate with cut eggs and enjoy.

What a great way to start a meal!

How to boil eggs and peel them easily
Put room temperature eggs into a pot of tepid water and bring to a rapid boil. Turn off the heat and let sit 8 minutes. Cool off in cold water and let sit five more minutes. The shell will be easy to remove and comes off without a fuss. I use fresh from the farm eggs despite a belief that older eggs peel easier.

Ode to the Farmer's Market, a rant

For the past year my family has lived more 'locally' and 'in the season' than ever before. It wasn't an act of culinarian defiance or even a misguided political statement. It simply was the continued evolution of what we have been doing for the last decade. Without intending to, our family's diet has become hyper seasonal, consuming a wider range of vegetables more intensely than any time before.

I used to ponder at length why vegetables just tasted so much better in France than here. Eat at almost any restaurant or stop at any town market, buy something and you'll see and taste what I mean. Zucchini tastes like the perfect zucchini and carrots like the perfect carrot. How could one country do that so consistently across the board? Then it hit me like an errant lightning strike on a bright sunny day. Food grown and eaten in due season simply tastes better. I was halfway through a plateful of artichokes barigoule when I had what I am now terming my artichoke epiphany. I started to notice how much better the artichokes I bought from Patreece at DeNoble Farms tasted than I ever remembered before. Certainly better than the overpriced, dead looking ones found at my neighborhood grocery store. As I ate, I awoke to the fact that artichokes eaten this time of year are more tender and have no choke to remove; leaving them almost completely edible. I bought bigs ones, little ones, even their five dollar bags of golf ball sized artichokes. Every week for the past month I bought so many artichokes that the girls who worked the farmer's market asked if I was buying them for a restaurant. Truth is, I simply cannot stop eating them.

A large part of the problem is the way we have industrialized and corporatized our food system. Vegetables are grown on enormous farms, with lots of harmful chemicals, mechanically picked green and shipped thousands of miles before they end up on your plate. Grocery stores are teeming with an insipid, varietal deprived mono-culture of fruits and vegetables devoid of flavor with an equally suspicious lifespan. Sadly most Americans have grown accustomed to the system and forgotten what real vegetables taste like or even that there used to be an infinite amount of apple varieties to choose from.

Thankfully there has been a green revolution brewing quietly under our noses. More people are demanding to know the provenance of their food and whether or not it has been genetically modified. Buying local has become a rallying cry. The fight to have food labeled is now national news. I see more locally grown food offered in the produce section of large chains. More farmers markets are appearing on the landscape offering a more diverse selection of products. I can buy spigarello and espelette peppers at my local market. People are producing artisan foods ranging from kim chee and cheeses to a wide range of charcuterie, extruded pastas and kombuchas. It gives me hope. I have developed a personal standard for buying food for my family. I want to know the name of the person who raised my food. Whether or not it is certified organic means less to me than whether it is chemical free and local. I enjoy taking my son to visit small farms and orchards to see first hand where our food comes from. I want him to reconnect and hold communion with the Earth.

"The first supermarket supposedly appeared on the American landscape in 1946. That is not very long ago. Until then, where was all the food? Dear folks, the food was in homes, gardens, local fields, and forests. It was near kitchens, near tables, near bedsides. It was in the pantry, the cellar, the backyard."

— Joel Salatin

Roasted Beet Salad

Feta Cheese, Oranges, Pistachios and Young Arugula

This salad has greatly evolved throughout my career. Its roots lie in the beloved 1990's warm goat cheese salad with roasted beets popular on everyone's menus. Slowly but surely the dish changed as I moved from one kitchen to another. Most ingredients were replaced by ones more native or available to where I lived. In my last kitchen, I found myself working in Southern California at a great, yet tragically short lived, Mediterranean restaurant. Even in the Desert, there was an abundance of local ingredients that influenced this dish. We had several orange trees growing in our parking lot alongside figs and olives. Sicilian green pistachios seemed more in line than the walnuts I had been using up to that point. Fig vincotto replaced the reduced Balsamic vinegar. The final change occurred when a local vendor turned me onto a super creamy Bulgarian Feta. The metamorphosis was complete, a new dish born. . . . . . .

Baking Beets

8 beets, use different colors
1 tablespoon olive oil
2 teaspoons herbes de Provence
1 teaspoon sea salt

Making the Salad

3 tablespoons sunflower seed oil
2 teaspoons flaky sea salt
2 teaspoons piment d'ville
4 ounces feta cheese chunks
2 oranges, segmented
20 shelled green pistachios, crushed
2 ounces young arugula
2 tablespoons fig vincotto

Baking Beets

Toss beets in olive oil, herbes de Provence and sea salt. Put on a baking sheet wrapped in aluminum foil. Roast at 350 degrees till a knife easily penetrates the flesh, about 90 minutes. Remove and let cool to room temperature.

Making the Salad

Peel and slice beets. Separately toss each color of beets in a bowl with sunflower seed oil, flaky sea salt and piment d'ville. Arrange in a circle ringing the edge of a plate. Toss feta chunks, orange segments, pistachios and arugula together. Plate in the center of the beets. Drizzle fig vincotto over and enjoy!

A Note about Ingredients

Fig vincotto is made from freshly pressed grape juice slowly reduced with figs till very thick, sweet and concentrated. Vincotto adds a flavorful sweet note to grilled meats, salads and anything you drizzle it over. For the most part one ingredient can always be substituted for another. This is how new dishes are created. Do not get locked into the dogma that prevents experimentation. If you can't find piment d'ville, use Aleppo peppers or something else. If you can't find fig vincotto, substitute apple balsamic or balsamic glaze. The only constant in life is change.

Roasted Peppers
Stuffed with fresh Goat Cheese, Anchoïade Sauce

A really simple dish that has all the elements of Provence hidden within its layers. Smoky, roasted peppers married with wild dried herbs, pungent garlic, anchovies and creamy goat cheese. Almost something I would expect a shepherd to make for his evening supper in the rugged hills over a wood fire. It makes a wonderful appetizer or a great meal, especially paired with a big green salad. Anchovies are an interesting thing in American culture. While French people revel at its wonderful pungent, briny flavors, most Americans recoil in horror at the very thought. I got to the point where I stopped mentioning the anchovy part and let people be persuaded by the seductive flavors. Even if you consider yourself an anchovy hater I suggest you try this dish. . . . .

Stuffed Peppers
4 fire roasted peppers
8 ounces fresh goat cheese
10 basil leaves, chopped
1 teaspoon herbes de Provence
1 clove garlic, mashed
1 teaspoon flake sea salt

Anchoïade
10 anchovy fillets
2 egg yolks
1/2 lemon, juiced
1 small clove of mild garlic, chopped
1/2 cup mild olive oil
2 teaspoons anchovy oil

Stuffed Peppers
Make a slit lengthwise in the roasted peppers and remove as many seeds as you can without fully opening the pepper. If a few remain it only adds to the rustic nature of this dish. Try to preserve its form as best as possible.

Mix the goat cheese, basil, herbes de Provence, garlic and salt together. Use a pastry bag to pipe the goat cheese mixture into peppers.

Lay the peppers down, cut side hidden from view in an oven proof dish lubricated with a small amount of olive oil. Roast at 400 degrees till hot and bubbly, about ten minutes.

Anchoïade
While the peppers are roasting, make the anchoïade. Put anchovies in the bowl of your food processor. Add the egg yolks, lemon juice and garlic. Puree till sort of smooth. It's ok if there are anchovy lumps left. With the motor still running, slowly drizzle in the olive oil and anchovy oil in a thin stream. The sauce will thicken as the oil is incorporated. If it gets too thick, simply add a spoonful or two of hot water to thin the sauce to a pourable state.

Easily Skin a Pepper
Burn pepper skins off by placing them directly on a burner and cooking till the skins turn jet black. You will need to keep rotating the pepper to blacken evenly. I never tried an electric stove before now. I currently live in a home with an electric range and had to try. I used a painter's blowtorch to speed up the process because I am impatient. A true MacGyver moment if there ever was one. The show must go on and sometimes our best skill is improvisation.

"Cooking is not complicated. You have to be well organized, to remember things, and to have a bit of taste. I learned to cook by doing it, simple as that."
– Eugenie Brazier

Mussels 'Pastis'

Spanish Chorizo, Leeks and Piquillo Peppers

This recipe was born during the early days of Pili Pili in Chicago when I was looking for classic recipes I could modify for the American palate. To get the creative juices flowing, I would drink a Pastis and watch Marcel Pagnol movies late into the night. Part of the development process is getting into character and thoroughly thinking a concept out. I imagined I was visiting Marseille and eating mussels: How would they be served? What would they taste like? What would be served alongside? I closed my eyes and imagined the smells, sounds and flavors of the Old Port. I felt myself sitting outside watching the commotion of commerce unfold. I imagined a steaming bowl of mussels served by a gregarious waiter in a long, flowing black apron and white shirt. Confidently lifting the searing top off, as he had done so many times before. He no longer felt the pain in his calloused hands, but welcomed it. The sweet, salty scents of licorice, shellfish and spicy cured pork released into the air on billowy currents of steam. Eyes closed in ecstasy as the first mussels are being savored. Crusty, warm bread patiently awaits its turn to swim in the broth. . . . .

2.5 pounds mussels, cleaned
3 tablespoons of unsalted butter
2 cloves garlic, mashed
1 thin leek, cleaned and diced
1 piquillo pepper, diced
4 ounces Spanish chorizo, diced
1 cup white wine
1/2 cup Pastis
1/2 cup heavy cream
2 tablespoons chopped parsley
pinch of sea salt and black pepper

Use a pan large enough to comfortably hold the mussels. Melt the butter and cook garlic till the aromas are released. Add the leek, piquillo pepper and chorizo. Continue cooking for a few moments till the leeks soften. Add your wine, Pastis and cream and bring to a full boil. Add the cleaned mussels, cover the pot tightly and steam till they all are open. Discard any that do not open. Mix in chopped parsley and taste your mussel broth. Season with sea salt and pepper. You may or may not need salt; It depends on the salinity of your mussels. Serve immediately in the pot with a bowl for shells.

Cleaning mussels: *My new favorite mussels come from Saltspring Island in British Columbia. The massive mussels have a bright salinity and a sweet ocean flavor that is addictive. You need to clean your mussels before using them. I usually wait till the last absolute moment keeping them alive as long as possible. Scour the shells with a clean stainless steel scrubby to remove any sea plants stuck to the shells. There may be a hairy fiber sticking out. This is called the beard. It is how mussels attach themselves to things underwater so they aren't washed away by the tide. Grab hold of the beard and pull it out firmly. If your mussels are extremely fresh, you may be involved in a tug of war. Keep mussels submerged in a bowl of very cold water while getting everything else ready.*

Cleaning leeks: *Not much can be worse than eating a beautiful dish and chewing on gritty leeks. While working for Chef Louis Szathmary in Chicago in the mid 1980's, I learned a trick for easily cleaning the dirt and grit out of leeks. Dice the leeks and soak in a large bowl of cold water. Add a tablespoon of salt and agitate the water. The salt acts as an abrasive and removes the grit. The sand will settle to the bottom of the bowl. Scoop leeks out of water and use. Do not pour the leeks and water into a strainer. If you do that you are pouring the sand back over the leeks.*

Marseille Fish Soup
Rouille, Garlic Croûtons and Gruyère

Marseille fish soup, or soupe de poissons as it is called in the South of France, is something I actually yearn for. The rich, assertive flavors redolent with the very soul of Provence takes me to the old port of Marseille where I first tried it. Nothing could be more Provençal than to eat a fish soup, whether it is bouillabaisse, bourride or a simple one like this. Make a big batch and freeze what you don't eat. Trust me, you will thank me for this advice. . . . .

Soup Base
1/2 cup olive oil
2 sweet onions, sliced
1/2 bulb fennel, chopped
6 cloves garlic, mashed
enough fresh hot pepper, see Chef's
    Note below
1 bay leaf
2 teaspoons saffron
1 Dungeness crab, crushed into small
    pieces
28 ounce can San Marzano tomatoes
¼ cup Pastis
2 pounds fish fillets, see sidebar below

Finishing the Soup
1 cup rouille, see page 39
16 croûtons rubbed with garlic
1 cup grated Gruyère

Chef's Note: I love to use fresh Espelette pepper for the soup base. It has the perfect level of heat. Just hot enough to feel the burn, but not so hot that it causes pain. You can use jalapeños, or whatever pepper catches your fancy. Start with smaller amounts to test your threshold of heat.

Soup Base
Heat the olive oil in a large, heavy gauge pot. Sauté sliced onions and fennel until softened and translucent, about five minutes. Add mashed garlic, hot pepper, bay leaf, saffron and crab. Continue cooking till the pleasant aromas of garlic fill your kitchen and the crab shells begin to turn red.

Crush the tomatoes and add along with their juice, Pastis and the fish fillets. Add enough cold water to cover everything by an inch. Bring to a boil, then lower and simmer for thirty minutes.

Strain the broth, saving the solids to pass through a food mill. Pick out the larger pieces of crab shell. They tend to get stuck in the mill. Food mills are great kitchen tools to puree homemade tomato sauces and mashed potatoes while aerating the finished product. The body and flavor of the soup comes from the proteins that get passed through and added back to the broth. Look at the picture on the facing page. You will notice the coarse appearance caused by tiny bits of fish proteins suspended in the soup. I love the rustic appeal of this soup.

Finishing the Soup
Adjust the seasonings and serve in heated bowls. Pass around bowls of grated Gruyère, toasted croûtons and rouille. The best way to enjoy is to put a dollop of rouille on a croûton and float it in the soup then sprinkle with Gruyère.

Which Fish to Use
Fish soup is economically made in the coastal regions of France because of the abundance of small rock fish to flavor the broth. Buy inexpensive mild fish like trout, shrimp or snapper that are prevalent in your market. It will change the flavor but still capture the essence.

Bourride

Provençal Sunshine: Codfish, Shrimp, Mussels, Saffron Orange Broth

Marinated fish

1 pound codfish, cut in four
½ pound bay scallops
1 pound Manila clams, scrubbed
½ pound shrimp, peeled
¼ cup olive oil
2 cloves garlic, chopped
1 big pinch saffron
1 small handful basil
1 orange, zested/juiced
¼ cup pastis

Broth

½ fennel bulb, julienned
½ onion, sliced
2 carrots, julienned
½ red pepper, julienned
4 cloves garlic, chopped
2 teaspoons saffron
4 San Marzano tomatoes, chopped
2 cups white wine
1 quart fish broth
½ cup Pastis

Rouille

2 egg yolks
2 teaspoons sea salt
Large pinch saffron
2 teaspoons sweet paprika
2 garlic cloves
1 tablespoon Sriracha hot sauce
2 teaspoons red vinegar
½ cup canola oil

When you are ready to eat

2 egg yolks
16 slices of French bread, toasted

Marinated fish

Place all seafood into a non-reactive bowl and toss with olive oil, garlic, saffron, basil, orange zest, orange juice and Pastis. Chop any fennel fronds and toss with seafood. Marinate fish overnight.

Broth

Sauté fennel, onion, carrots, and pepper in olive oil till soft with no color, about 5 minutes. Add garlic and saffron and cook till fragrant, about one minute. Add tomatoes, white wine, fish broth and Pastis, bring to a boil then simmer for thirty minutes. Chill broth overnight.

Rouille

To make the Rouille, put the egg yolks, sea salt, saffron, paprika, garlic cloves, Sriracha and vinegar into your food processor and puree till smooth. Slowly add oil till very thick. Adjust seasonings to your taste and chill overnight.

When you are ready to eat

Bring the broth to a boil, add seafood and marinade and cook till done, about five to ten minutes depending on the thickness of the seafood. Nicely arrange seafood in a serving tureen. Whisk together an egg yolk and ½ cup of Rouille. Ladle in one cup of hot fish soup and whisk till smooth and creamy. Whisk the egg mixture into the pot then pour over fish in tureen.

Serve with toasted French bread and Rouille on the side.

Fish Stock

Fish stock is simply made by sautéing 2 sliced sweet onions, 1 leek and two ribs of celery in butter. Add two rinsed fish bones, 1/2 bottle white wine, 2 quarts water, a few sprigs of aromatic herbs like thyme, bay leaf and tarragon and a teaspoon of black peppercorns. Bring to a boil, then turn off and let sit 45 minutes. Strain and keep the liquid.

The Origins of Bourride

I am surely going to piss off my Marseille family and bouillabaisse purists alike with this one. To put it simply, bourride is bouillabaisse's troubled half-sister. While they certainly share a common lineage, there are stark characteristics that differentiate the two. Classically, both start with a pureed broth made from onions, fennel, garlic, orange peel, saffron, tomatoes, olive oil and small rock fish.

Traditionally bourride is an emulsified fish broth made from small unsellable rock fish thickened with Aioli. I prefer making a lighter broth and thickening with rouille to give an extra kick. Provençal flavors are meant to be bigger, bolder and more assertive than in other parts of France. Rouille just adds an extra kick I love. I make the broth by leaving the vegetables julienned and omitting sieved rock fish. Louis Szathmary, an early mentor once said "people do not eat methods, people eat results." The result is an easy to make, sharable version of a Provençal classic.

Eating bouillabaisse is a carefully choreographed religious ceremony usually requiring 24 hour notice, whose consumption is performed in two sacred rites ending perhaps with genuflexion to the sacred cauldron. Bourride, on the other hand, is more like a courthouse marriage done on a whim over an office lunch break, still a covenant and very satisfying but with far less ceremony and planning.

Bouillabaisse is traditionally served in two courses starting with the broth ladled into warm bowls and served with garlic croûtons, shredded Parmesan, rouille and aioli. After seconds are offered, the whole fish poached in the broth are presented to the table, than filleted and served glistening in more broth. Bourride is made from fish fillets cooked in the broth and enriched by a liaison of egg yolks and aioli whisked in at the last moment. According to Alan Davidson in the 'Oxford Companion to Food', the first mention of a bouillabaisse-like soup of French origin appears in print in 'La Cuisine de Santé' authored by Jourdain Le Cointe in 1790. He describes a scene where fishermen and their wives are on a riverbed boiling a cauldron full of ingredients very reminiscent of bouillabaisse. The recipe given is called 'Matellote du Poisson'. It's not until 1830 when 'Le Cuisinier Durand' is written that we get a dish actually called bouillabaisse.

I started researching to find the earliest references of bourride and could not find anything earlier than Reboul's masterpiece 'La Cuisinière Provençale' written in 1897. Reboul describes a bouillabaisse made without saffron and thickened with aioli and egg yolks. I tried referencing food dictionaries and saw as many different versions as I had books, and I have over 2,000 cookbooks as of now. Many claim the only true bourride is made solely with monkfish in a white creamy sauce, possibly flavored with crushed fish liver. That local variation is properly called bourride setoise. I once had a prominent French Chef dining at my restaurant call me to his table to tell me although it was good, what I served was not a true bourride.

I started making bourride at the behest of Jacob, a lawyer/book dealer customer, at my first restaurant 'le Margaux' in 1993. I was in his bookshop looking for rare cookbooks and he told me of his favorite dish and asked if I had ever made it. I don't know why I lied, but I did. I replied with utmost confidence it was a specialty of mine and of course I'd be delighted to make it whenever he could get in. I secretly hoped that day would be far off enough to research and test it a few times. Unfortunately he made reservations for the next night and not only that, he was bringing eleven close friends. Panic struck as I combed through various cook books hoping to find at least two books corroborating the recipe. When I failed in that I figured the oldest book I owned probably was the closest to a true bourride so I settled on the 1938 version written in the Larousse Gastronomique. I followed the three paragraph recipe with my Provençale mother's irreverence to measurement and thankfully impressed Jacob. I have continued to make bourride and think of Jacob every single time.

Cured Black Cod
Fried Chickpeas, Piquillos, Chorizo Croquettes and Anchoïade

Every dish is a reflection of the moment: an edible photograph of a Chef's mind. This dish is the unexpected collaboration of chefs David Everitt-Matthias and my Sous Keith Schneider. A dish born out of the circumstances of the moment. I bought Chef Everitt-Matthias's book 'Essence' years ago and oodled over the gorgeous photography and even better recipes. I couldn't afford to get to his restaurant in England so I started mimicking some of his dishes. I ran a straight copy of David's 'home-salted cod with roasted tomatoes, chickpeas and anchovy dressing' so long I started thinking it was mine. The flavors and scents spoke of the history of Provence. Wisps of the citrus cure made me feel like I was standing in Menton, the pearl of France, located on the Italian border long known for its superior lemons, oranges and tangerines. I added Keith's chorizo croquettes because I love the play on flavors of mixing spicy pork and fish together. . . . .

Cure
1 ounce sea salt
2 teaspoons sugar
1 orange, zested
1 teaspoon herbes de Provence
4 - 4 ounce pieces black cod

Finishing the Dish
1 tablespoon unsalted butter
1 tablespoon olive oil
12 piquillo peppers, drained
60 cooked chickpeas, drained
4 ounces arugula
4 small chorizo croquettes, next page
Anchoïade sauce, see page 32

Cure
Mix the salt, sugar, orange zest and herbes de Provence well. Pack the salt on all four pieces of cod and let cure for no more than three hours. If you leave it on too long the salt will penetrate the meat and make it too salty.

Finishing the Dish
Rinse cure off black cod. Sauté over high heat skin side down in a mixture of butter and olive oil till brown and crispy, about five minutes. The skin will naturally want to curl as it cooks. Remedy that by pressing the cod flat with a pair of tongs or a metal spatula. Flip over and continue cooking on low heat till fish is fully cooked, about five minutes. Black cod is a very moist and forgiving fish. A perfect fish for forgetful cooks. Remove fish and drain on a paper towel.

Sauté piquillo peppers in the fish pan till warmed through. Fry chickpeas in same oil as croquettes till brown and crispy.

Arrange a small pile of arugula on a plate. Top with piquillo peppers and black cod. Arrange croquettes and fried chickpeas on plate and finish by drizzling anchoïade over.

Salt Cod
Salt Cod is the first commercially fished commodity after the dark ages. The French led the world in the curing of cod and had strong reservoirs enabling them to sell to their neighbors. Salt Cod popularity was because of its ability to keep for long periods of time.

Chorizo Croquettes

Liquid center Spanish Chorizo croquette with Rouille

Keith Schneider was my last Sous Chef in the professional world. He looked like a young Michael Douglas and made the best creamy, liquid center croquettes on the planet. Five years sweating in Iron Chef Jose Garces' kitchens paid off. The first dish I tasted was a variation of this croqueta served with a saffron aioli. I loved it so much I immediately put it on the menu. You can substitute almost anything for the chorizo to make other croquettes. . . . .

Chorizo croquettes

4 ounces unsalted butter
4 ounces Spanish chorizo, finely chopped
1 - 1/2 cups milk
2 envelops gelatin
1/3 cup flour
2 tablespoons parsley

Bread and fry

1 cup flour
2 eggs, beaten
2 cups Panko
10 cups frying oil

Rouille, see page 39

Chorizo Croquettes start to finish

Melt butter and mix with chorizo and cook for five minutes. While that is cooking, mix milk and powdered gelatin. Let it sit for five minutes. Add flour to chorizo and cook over low heat constantly stirring with a wooden spoon for three minutes. Whisk in milk mixture. Keep whisking as the milk gets super thick, about five minutes. Add parsley then pour into an 8 inch by 8 inch glass dish and refrigerate for two hours or until solidified. Cut out four circles with a cookie cutter or water glass. Save the rest for snacking on.

Put flour, beaten eggs and panko into three separate bowls. Dip croquette first in the flour, then egg and finally in the panko. Make sure you coat them well or they will disintegrate in the hot oil.

Heat frying oil to 350 degrees. Carefully drop croquettes into hot oil. Deep fry croquettes till brown and crispy, about five minutes. Serve with rouille!

Simple grilled Loup de Mer
served with Artichokes Barigoule and Olive Tapenade

One of the great joys in the South of France is to grill fish over dried fennel branches. It was a near mythical dish spoken in hushed tones in my home growing up. As a child I believed in two things, Santa Claus and grilled Loup. Every time my mother and I get together the focus is always food. We plan entire vacations around where and what we will eat. My mother came to visit recently and we took a trip into the woods surrounding Oregon's Mount Hood. I found a campsite along a small river to provide the perfect backdrop to our picnic. Good food can happen anywhere and under any circumstance. Free yourself from the bondage that food is a chore. There is no greater act than sharing a wonderful meal with people you love. If you are lucky to live in parts of the country like Northern California where wild fennel grows rampant, simply cut it down and let dry in the sun. Get your coals white hot and put dried fennel branches on top. Licorice smoky flavors will pleasantly permeate your fish and lend a feeling of being in Provence. Do not be a slave to the recipe; if you don't have dried fennel, grill over coals anyway. This dish is perhaps the best thing I cook. . . . .

Accompaniments
tapenade, see page 10
artichokes barigoule, see page 85
1/4 cup basil, rough chopped

Loup de Mer
2 Loup de Mer
2 sprigs thyme
1 lemon, sliced thin
sea salt and black pepper
fruity French olive oil

Accompaniments
Pour yourself a big glass of Pastis, put on some French music and let the spirit of Provence fill your soul. Put the tapenade into a rustic bowl and set on your table. Gently heat the artichokes barigoule and garnish with fresh cut basil.

Loup de Mer
Get your coals white hot. Lay the Loup on a board in front of you. Put a thyme sprig and three slices of lemon in the cavity. Season with sea salt and black pepper. Drop the fish on the grill and let it cook. Fight the urge to prematurely turn it. Let it get good and crispy on one side then flip over. The best part is the crunchy skin. The second side cooks quickly. Put Loup on a plate and spoon a few tablespoons of artichoke broth over. Drizzle with fruity olive oil and the accompaniments on the side.

Not-So-Simple Loup de Mer

Roast Sea Bass, Swiss Chard, Tomato Confit, Saffron Sauce

Loup de mer, otherwise known as branzino or sea bass depending on whatever country you're from or where you've had it first. It's a wildly popular Mediterranean fish that's easy to find on menus across America. Its undying popularity dates back to when man first started recording his impressions of food onto paper. Pliny instructs us that Loup from the rivers is superior to ones from the sea. Nowadays most loup found in America comes from fish farms in Greece. It has a firm textured white flesh that can take almost any preparation in stride. This recipe originated as one for sardines by the celebrated Chef Alain Ducasse. . . . .

Stuffing for Fish

1 bunch Swiss chard
1 egg, beaten
1/2 cup Parmesan
2 cups panko
1/2 cup heavy cream
24 cherry tomatoes confit, see page 73
16 cloves roasted garlic, see warm olive
    recipe page 13
2 tablespoons basil, sliced thin

Stuffing the Loup

2 loup de mer, 1.5# each
sea salt and white pepper

Finishing the Dish

4 tablespoons unsalted butter
1 cup white wine sauce, see below
pinch saffron

Stuffing for Fish

Blanch Swiss chard leaves in rapidly boiling salted water for three minutes and then drain. Quickly cool off in ice water. Squeeze leaves dry, trim stems off and rough chop. Slice the stems thinly, reserving them for assembling the dish later.

Mix the Swiss chard leaves, beaten egg, Parmesan, panko, cream, 8 cherry tomatoes, 12 cloves of garlic and basil. Let sit till the panko rehydrates and all the moisture has been absorbed, about 20 minutes.

Stuffing the Loup

Either ask your fish monger to fillet or arm yourself with a sharp knife and fillet your own. Season the fillets with sea salt and pepper. Divide the stuffing into four balls. Wrap the fillet around each ball with the skin side facing out. Tie each fillet snugly with a piece of cotton kitchen twine.

Finishing the Dish

Lay the Loup on a piece of buttered parchment paper and roast at 400 degrees, basting often with butter. Flip after seven minutes and cook till firm and lightly browned, about another seven minutes. Sauté Swiss chard stems in roasting pan. Spoon in center of warmed plate and top with fish. Heat white wine sauce mixed with saffron until simmering. Spoon sauce around fish and garnish with remaining cherry tomatoes and roasted garlic.

White Wine Sauce

A multi purpose Mother sauce I use for a lot of dishes, white wine sauce is made by sautéing three sliced shallots in one tablespoon of unsalted butter for five minutes. Add one cup white wine, a sprig of thyme and a bay leaf and reduce by fifty percent. Add one cup chicken or fish stock and reduce by fifty percent. Add one cup of heavy cream and reduce to sauce consistency. Strain sauce and whisk in four tablespoons of unsalted butter.

Albacore Tuna and Mussels 'Marseille Style'

Seared Tuna, Mussels, Olives, Capers, Tomato Sauce

This is my spin on a classic Southern French preparation for tuna. I started adding mussels when I discovered ones from Saltspring Island in British Columbia. They are the best mussels available in the US market. . . . .

24 ounces tuna, cut into eight pieces
sea salt and black pepper
1 teaspoon herbes de Provence
1 tablespoon olive oil
1 tablespoon unsalted butter
1 clove garlic, mashed
pinch piment d'ville
1 cup white wine
1 pound mussels, cleaned, see page 35
1 cup tomato sauce, see page 90
pinch saffron
1/4 cup Niçoise olives
1 tablespoon capers
8 basil leaves, torn into pieces
one tablespoon unsalted butter

I fluctuate between using day boat caught, local Garibaldi, Oregon albacore tuna and the more commonly available ahi tuna. Either works well. Use whatever looks best in your market.

Season tuna with sea salt, black pepper and herbes de Provence. Sear tuna in smoking hot olive oil in a non stick pan. Remove from pan and reserve. Add butter, mashed garlic, piment d'ville and white wine. Steam cleaned mussels till they open. Discard any that do not open. Use a slotted spoon to remove mussels. Keep mussels warm with reserved tuna. Add tomato sauce, saffron, olives and capers. Bring to a boil then lower to a simmer. Adjust salt and pepper to taste. Add basil leaves and butter. Just before serving add the tuna and mussels back. The heat of the sauce will gently warm the tuna and finished cooking it. Tuna should always be served cooked no more than rare to medium rare or it will dry out.

A Simple Roast Chicken
Ten Easy Rules for a Perfect Chicken

The quest: a perfect simple roast chicken. A humble and deeply satisfying dish but somehow as elusive as a unicorn or five leaf clover. How hard can it really be to roast a simple chicken? Not hard if you follow a few simple rules. . . . . .

The general rules of proper roasting and eating of chicken:

1. Pick a free range bird about 3.5 pounds who is fed either an organic or natural diet.

2. Preheat your oven to 425 degrees. Let warm up all the way before cooking bird.

3. Season chicken with liberal amounts of sea salt, black pepper, herbs de Provence and piment d'ville or espelette pepper. Don't worry conservative friends, here is the chance where liberal does good for you too. I promise Rush won't kick you out of the Ditto club. Be sure to heavily salt the opening of the cavity. These are the crispiest pieces of crackly crispy chicken and, in my humble opinion, the true reward of whomever gets to bone the bird.

4. Stuff half a lemon, a whole head of garlic cut in two and more fresh thyme and rosemary than you think. The lemon perfumes the bird in such a pleasant and nuanced way. Cooking is about building subtle layers that are almost imperceptible.

5. Put a wire rack on a cookie sheet or sheet pan and roast bird 40 minutes breast side down. Yes, set your damned kitchen timer for this one, it's science.

6. Flip over and roast another full 40 minutes breast side up.

7. Stand bird up with legs flailing in the air for 20 minutes before you cut the bird. The juices will redistribute throughout the bird and keep it juicy beyond imagination. Do not give into temptation, be strong.

8. Always roast a whole bird. It is silly, more expensive and wasteful not to do the whole bird. You will end up with enough meals for a few days and two to three quarts of homemade chicken broth.

9. Cut the breasts, wings, legs and thighs off. If you are smart you will eat both 'oysters' before anyone notices. The oysters are the tenderest piece of chicken that are located where the thigh bone connects to the carcass. Shh, don't tell anyone.

10. Eat the breast the first day then the dark meat the second. It almost sounds like a commandment so abide by it. The dude does... And on the second day, God said... The breast comes out of the oven so beautifully juicy and tender yet somehow loses that quality by day two.

11. Immediately make a chicken stock with the carcass, herbs and lemon. It will be so superior to any store bought chicken stock and far more useful and healthful.

Classics can be phenomenal when done right. A simple roast chicken dish could be the best thing you ever eat.
— Joe Bastianich

A Rant about Chicken Stock

Many years ago I graduated from the prestigious New England Culinary Institute run by Chef Michel LeBorgne, a hard-nosed Frenchman from Northern France. Like every great Chef before him, and probably every one since, Chef LeBorgne had his aphorisms that we metered our lives by. They were relentlessly repeated as we chopped vegetables, sautéed fish and made stocks. Each one growled required the standard "oui Chef" shouted back in unison like recruits at boot camp.

Most were modified from the classic themes of how older generations had it much harder than us young worthless punks. "We were so poor as apprentices, we only had one pair of shoes between the two of us" or "I used to walk to the restaurant uphill both ways." The one that stuck and became part of my own repertoire was "I lost my first million in the garbage can". That line inspired me throughout my career and helped maintain very low food costs. Even now, decades later, I am still haunted by that principal.

More and more of us are rediscovering the healthy advantages of home cooking and eating whole unprocessed foods. Local farmer's markets make the availability of grass fed meats, wild fish, vegetables and fruits more accessible. Authors like Michael Pollan remind us eating smaller amounts of protein and larger amounts of vegetables is better for us. The transition back to cooking and eating properly can benefit from some sage Chef wisdom.

Home cooks always seem to be looking for an easier, faster ways to cook things. Sometimes quick and easy really isn't quick, easy or even cheaper. One thing that amazes me is the proliferation of four dollar quart sized tetra paks of stocks. God knows I have used countless quarts over the years. I started reading the ingredient lists and was appalled to find that even the organic ones contained ingredients like 'natural chicken flavor' and more salt than you could imagine. Do your own research on what natural chicken flavor means; I'll give you a hint, it's not chicken.

Michel LeBorgne's line kept popping back into my mind. I had lived that aphorism for so many years as Chef and never thought about its application at home. One of my pet peeves was the amount of waste in kitchens. I did a few day consulting gig for a terribly run restaurant in Southern California. I watched in utter disbelief as a cook trimmed chicken wings off whole chickens and threw them away literally five feet from another cook opening bags of frozen wings used for a popular appetizer. The irony was unbearable.

In my kitchens, my crew was taught to save vegetable trimmings for use in the countless stocks that quietly simmer around the clock in professional kitchens. Every day we would go through 50 pound bags of carrots, sacks of onions, cases of celery and pounds of fresh herbs. A million dollars in the garbage happens way quicker than most people think. Every penny saved is a penny more of profit.

I started applying that concept in my own home. I keep a stainless steel bowl in my freezer. Every time I peel a carrot, garlic or an onion I add the peelings to it. After a week it fills up. The most commonly used vegetable peelings that end up in there are fresh herbs (thyme, tarragon, chives and rosemary), celery, garlic, tomatoes and sweet peppers. When you are ready to make a stock and feel you need more vegetables, then add more. Don't stress, whatever you do at home is infinitely better than buying pre-made stuff.

We eat one to two roast chickens per week and all the carcasses get saved for stock. When you think about it, buying a whole chicken is a smarter and cheaper choice. One whole organic chicken cost me around 10 to 12 dollars. I get five to six servings of food out of it and about three quarts of stock. The value of the stock alone is $12 if you buy a comparable amount of tetra paks.

Making great chicken stock at home is super easy, requires almost no effort, and will save you lots of money. Consuming bone broth, or stock, is widely gaining in popularity as quite a few nationally recognized Chefs began promoting what our ancestors already knew: bone broth is great for you. It rids the body of toxins, strengthens joints, heals your gut and boosts collagen just to name a few. I use stock for pan steaming both my morning and dinner vegetables. I use it for quick sauces for my lunchtime proteins and I absolutely adore soups. The use for stocks is unlimited and easily provides a lot of umami to home cooking. Most days I have a stock pot sitting on my stove bubbling away, filling my home with delicious scents and my tummy with great flavors!

HOMEMADE CHICKEN STOCK

1 chicken carcass, including all trimmings and fat
4 ribs celery, washed and rough chopped
6 carrots, washed and rough chopped
2 onions, chopped
1 head garlic, cut in half
1 bunch thyme (add tarragon, rosemary, chive if you like)
1 bay leaf
20 peppercorns
cold water to cover

INSTRUCTIONS

Put everything in a large pot, cover with cold water, bring to a boil and then simmer for a minimum of 6 hours and sometimes a full 24 hours on low heat. Strain through a fine meshed strainer and freeze in recycled glass jars. Remember liquids expand as they freeze so do not fill jars fully.

Recipes are nothing more than guidelines.
Experiment to find what flavors you like most.

Provençal Truffles, Leeks, Carrots & Foie Gras

Chicken in Half Mourning, a luxurious yet simple chicken preparation, was popularized by Mere Brazier in the 1920's. The term "Mères Lyonnaises", or mothers of Lyon (France), refers to a long lineage of female Chefs beginning in the mid 1700's who brought the gastronomic spotlight to Lyon, the undisputed gastronomical capital of France. Their influence and impact helped define and shape classic French cooking in modern times. Eugenie held the record for being the first Chef with two simultaneous three star Michelin restaurants. I have been making my own version slightly modified from her recipe. It is my tribute to her brilliance and her elegant simplicity.

Prepping the Chicken
2 whole fresh black truffles
1 chicken, weighing 3.5 pounds

Poaching the Chicken
2 tablespoons unsalted butter
1 leek, sliced thin and washed
2 carrots, peeled and sliced thin
1 sprig tarragon
1 spring thyme
1 bay leaf
2 teaspoons sea salt
1/2 teaspoons black pepper
2 quarts chicken stock
Foie Gras Sauce

Poaching Liquid
1/4 cup Madeira
truffle peelings
1/2 cup heavy cream
1/2 lemon or 1 tablespoon
   verjus
4 ounces grade b foie gras
flake sea salt
cracked black pepper

Prepping the chicken
Use a small paring knife to peel the thin outer layer of the truffle off. Reserve the peelings for the sauce. Cut the truffle into 1/8 inch slices. Use your fingertips to gently separate the chicken skin from the chicken meat. Gently tuck the truffle slices under the skin. The chicken will almost look black, like a woman in mourning. Let the chicken sit overnight to let the truffle flavors permeate the meat.

Poaching the Chicken
Find a sauce pot large enough to comfortably hold the chicken and all the chicken broth. Melt the butter and add the sliced leeks and carrots. Sauté for five or six minutes stirring constantly. Add the tarragon, thyme and bay leaf. While that is cooking, season the chicken with sea salt and black pepper. Add the chicken stock to the pot and bring to a rapid boil. Drop the chicken in and bring back to a boil. Reduce heat and gently poach for 40 minutes. Turn off the heat and let the chicken rest in the broth for an additional 30 minutes.

Crispy Duck Confit
Ratte Fingerling Potatoes, Olive Sauce

If I am able to choose my last meal than this is surely it. There is something especially comforting to me about duck confit. I love the fatty, crispy, salty explosion of flavors. Drink a beautiful Burgundy with this. As my friend Peter says, birds and Burgs. Truly a match made in Heaven. . . . .

For the Potatoes
1 pound freshly dug Ratte potatoes
1 bay leaf
1 sprig thyme
two whole garlic cloves, smashed
flaky sea salt

For the Duck Confit
4 duck legs, cooked confit style
1 cup duck fat

Finishing the Potatoes
1/2 cup duck fat
1 head garlic, peel and sliced thin
1 tablespoon fresh thyme
sea salt and black pepper

For the Olive Sauce
4 cups chicken stock, see page 57
1 tablespoon olive tapenade, see page 10

Duck Confit
4 duck legs
1/4 cup coarse sea salt
1 tablespoon black peppercorns
1 bunch thyme
1 bunch rosemary
1 sweet onion, unpeeled, sliced
1 head garlic, unpeeled, coarsely chopped
1 quart rendered duck fat

For the Potatoes
Scrub freshly dug Ratte potatoes to remove all dirt. Put into a four quart pan and cover with cold water. Add bay leaf, thyme sprig and garlic cloves. Season liberally with sea salt and bring to a boil. Reduce to a simmer and cook till tender, about ten minutes. You want the potatoes slightly firm. Remove potatoes to a strainer. When cool enough to touch without screaming, peel with a pairing knife and halve lengthwise. Pour a huge glass of wine and get ready for the meal of your life.

For the Duck Confit
Lay the duck confit in a pool of golden duck fat with the skin down. Turn the burner onto a medium flame and let cook slowly till the skin starts to crackle and turn brown. Low and slow is the method here. Keep legs warm while you finish the potatoes.

Finishing the Potatoes
Heat the golden duck fat till it is gently bubbling away. Add the halved Ratte potatoes and cook without flipping for ten minutes on medium to low heat. The idea is to cook till they appear almost withered and golden brown. Remove and drain from fat. Peel and slice an entire head of garlic. Yes an entire head. Pour about a ¼ cup of fat back into the pan. Add the garlic slices and cook on low heat stirring frequently. The idea is to slowly brown the garlic without burning. Burnt garlic tastes bitter and will kill the dish. If you do burn it, throw away before anyone notices. Chop fresh thyme leaves and toss with garlic. Add potatoes and keep tossing. Season with sea salt and black pepper.

For the Olive Sauce
Reduce 4 cups of home made chicken broth down to 1 cup of thick and concentrated liquid. Whisk in tapenade and rejoice in the world's simplest, most amazing sauce.

Finishing the Duck Confit
Season the duck legs with coarse sea salt. Mix the peppercorns, thyme, rosemary, sliced onion and coarsely chopped garlic. Pack around the duck legs and refrigerate for three days.

After the duck has marinated, wash legs off, immerse in duck fat and slow cook at 300 degrees in your oven till the duck meat just barely falls off the bone, about three hours. Cool immediately and leave in fat. The fat should cover the duck legs, preserving it in its golden depths. At this point I would consider vacuum packing the duck legs with a little of the fat for future use.

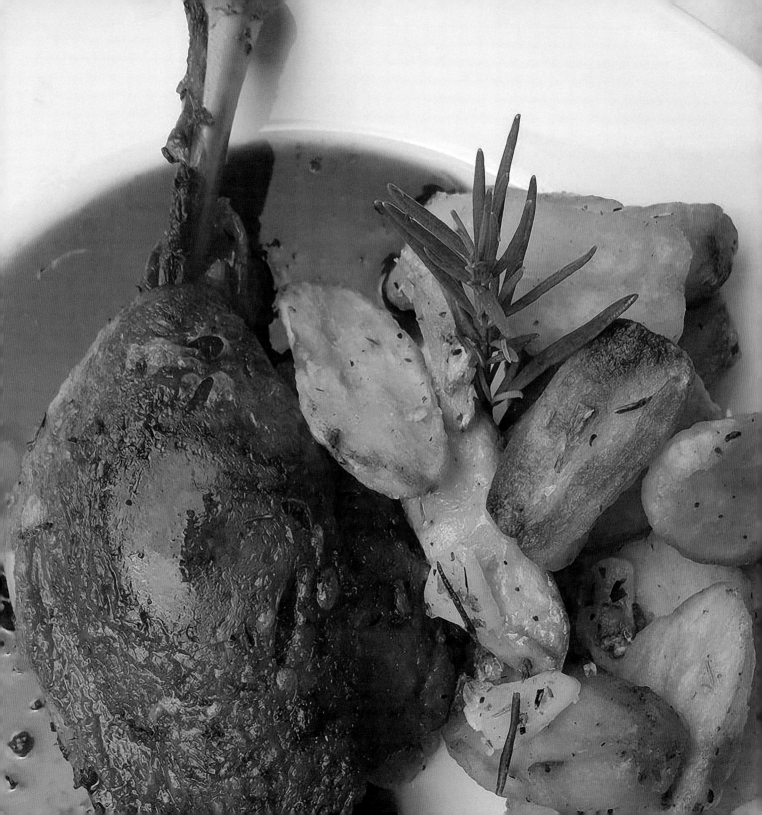

SuDan Farm

Finding great grass fed lamb is vital to my family's wellbeing. We eat lamb three times a week and I want to make sure what I put on my table is not only the healthiest, but the best tasting. As children you learn that you are what you eat. It is no different for animals. Grass fed lambs graze on big, wide open green pastures nibbling on lush grasses and wild herbs. As a consequence, they have higher Omega 3's and 3 to 5 times more CLA, conjugated linoleic acid, than traditionally raised commodity lamb. Omega 3's are an essential fatty acid necessary for human growth and development. CLA's have been proven to reduce cancer among many other significant benefits. Most importantly, grass fed lamb just tastes better than its more commercial cousin.

I discovered Dan and Sue Wilson's farm while wandering through the Portland Farmer's Market. I was in search of unctuous lamb cheeks to braise for our lunch and could not find them in any butcher shop in Portland. The sign for SuDan Farm caught my eye. It boasted a very long list of hard to find cuts like lamb sweetbreads, belly and trotter not to mention whole lamb shoulders, lamb jerky and the best 100% lamb sausages I have ever tried. The nice thing about Farmers markets is the direct relationship you can develop with the people that grow/raise your food. You can ask the farmer questions and learn about what and why they do what they do. I started buying so many lamb cheeks that they thought I was running a restaurant.

Their sustainably raised, grass fed lamb intrigued me so much I had to talk to Dan. He was very gracious and offered me to visit his farm. A few times a year they do 'open farms' and encourage visitors to flock to the farm to taste his lambs and learn about what they do. Dan says "the health and wellbeing of our animals is of the upmost importance to us. We regard them as our partners in life and business." They handle their farm like an open-source technology company where information is freely shared among different developers. This encourages better practices on land management, animal welfare and all the factors involved in creating a superior product.

Dan and Sue Wilson started their rural farm in 2000, in the historic community of Yoder, nine miles south of Canby, Oregon. He had walked away from a very successful career working for large agricultural corporation wanting to be his own boss. By 2001 he had assembled a few lambs old enough to process and started offering a small amount of cuts at a tiny booth at the Salem Farmers Market. They started raising hard to find breeds known for superior meat and breeding purposes like Border Leicester (English), Coopworth (New Zealand), and Gotland (Swedish) sheep. Over the next 14 years they have grown to where they now raise over 1,600 lamb per year, supplying many restaurants, grocery stores and customers. Nothing is wasted on a rural farm. His wife Sue further utilizes the lamb for producing yarns, blankets, sheepskins, felt and numerous other products for the fiber customers.

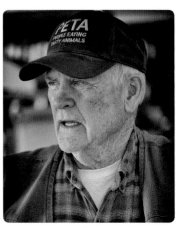

Dan Wilson

Grilled Lamb Chops
Lavender Honey and Herbes de Provence, Vegetable Tian

I try to buy everything we consume from small farmers, fishermen and foragers whom I know on a first name basis. Not only does it taste better, but it supports your local economy and keeps people in my community gainfully employed. We are blessed to live near the Portland farmer's market where we buy most of what we eat. Dan Wilson is a sheep farmer who raises some of the best grass fed lamb I've ever tasted. The love and care he raises his lamb with is evident in the flavor and texture of the finished meat. . . . .

Lavender Honey Brushed Lamb
2 racks of grass fed lamb
2 tablespoons lavender honey
2 teaspoons flaky sea salt
black pepper
2 teaspoons piment d'ville
2 teaspoons herbes de Provence

Vegetable Tian
2 Japanese eggplants
1/4 cup olive oil
2 thin golden summer squash
2 thin zucchini
1 cup tomato sauce, see page 90
2 sweet onions, sliced
2 tablespoons unsalted butter
1 bulb fennel, shaved thinly
8 plum tomatoes, sliced 1/4 inch thick
sea salt and black pepper
1 tablespoon thyme, chopped
2 tablespoons grated Parmesan

Chef's Note: *A lot of French dishes get their names from the vessel they are cooked in. Tians are earthen dishes used for cooking in Provence.*

Lavender Honey Brushed Lamb
Light a wood fire in your grill. While the wood is turning into coals, trim lamb rack into individual chops. Warm lavender honey and brush onto chops. Season liberally with salt, pepper, piment d'ville and herbes de Provence. Grill to whatever temperature you like.

Vegetable Tian
Slice eggplant thinly and soak in cold water for ten minutes. Soaking eggplant removes the bitter, astringent taste and helps prevent eggplant from soaking up all the oil. We were all taught to salt eggplants but I find this method more effective. Contrary to what your mind will tell you the eggplant does not get soggy. Drain, pat dry in a towel and sauté lightly in olive oil. Slice and lightly sauté summer squash and zucchini. Pour one cup of tomato sauce into an oven proof dish. Caramelize sliced onions in butter over high heat, about five minutes, then sprinkle over tomato sauce. Layer the squash, zucchini, shaved fennel, tomato and eggplant in the baking dish. Season with salt, pepper and thyme. Sprinkle with Parmesan and bake tian at 400 degrees for 20 minutes, or until hot.

the steps involved in assembling the tian

Roasted Lamb Hind Shanks

Scented with Rosemary and Dried Orange

I am a strong advocate of 100% grass fed lamb. It tastes better and is healthier than conventional lamb. It's sad we have to make the distinction between 100% grass fed and simply grass fed, but lawyers have gotten involved in our food chain. Pretty much any lamb that dreams of eating grass is technically grass fed. Grass fed, pasture raised and 100% natural are simply coded words used to confuse and deceive us. To be smart, skip the lawyers and buy your grass fed lamb from small producers like SuDan in Canby, Oregon. Every farmer's market I have been to has a lamb producer.

Lamb is one of the most neglected meats in the American diet. Sales have been a steady decline since World War II. In the 1960's, Americans ate 4.5 pounds of lamb per year. In 2013, it dropped to less than one pound per year. I eat one pound per week. Grass fed animals produce 500% more CLA, 400% more Vitamin A, 300 % more Vitamin E and 75% more Omega 3s than their conventionally fed counterparts.

Grass fed meats simply taste better. Remember, you are what you eat. We often forget the same applies with animals and seafood. In France, two areas are known for their widely superior lamb. The flocks in Sisteron (Provence) graze on grass pastures with lots of wild thyme and rosemary growing. The beautiful wild herbs perfume the meat. Perhaps the most coveted is the Agneau de pré-salé, or salt marsh lamb raised in Mont St. Michel. Blogger Helen Page writes "Mont-St-Michel Bay's extremely strong tides are well known. As a result of of the huge bay tides, the vegetation that grows here has had to adapt to life both above and below sea level. The subtle taste and tenderness of the meat from the lambs comes from the unique plants which thrive in environments with very high salt concentrations."

Whatever lamb you flock t'ewe, make sure it is grass fed! . . . .

4 grass fed lamb hind shanks
2 tablespoons herbes de Provence
1 tablespoon flaky sea salt
2 teaspoons black pepper
2 teaspoons piment d'ville
1/4 cup olive oil
4 heads of garlic
2 carrots, diced
1 sweet onion, diced
1 fennel bulb, diced
1 strip dried orange, see page 69
2 stalks of rosemary
1 cup white wine
1 cup water

Buy hind shanks as opposed to fore shanks. They are larger and far meatier. The ones I buy weigh almost 1.5 pounds each. You will have leftovers!

Preheat your oven to 450 degrees. Season shanks with herbes de Provence, sea salt, black pepper and piment d'ville. Find a roasting pan large enough to comfortably hold them. Put olive oil and lamb in and roast for 45 minutes turning once halfway through the cooking process.

Reduce the temperature to 350 degrees. Cut the garlic heads in half and add with all the remaining ingredients. Cover with aluminum foil and return to the oven. Braise for 2 hours, or until the meat is very tender and almost falling off the bone.

Serve on a platter with all the vegetables and cooking juices.

"Provençal cooking is not to put basil and garlic in everything, Not to put olive oil in everything."
- Gui Gedda

Provençal Lamb Daube 'Gui Gedda'

Grass fed Lamb Stew inspired by Chef Gui Gedda

Finding Gui Gedda's book 'Cooking School Provence' was a major find for me. I stumbled across it while searching for something else. I heard his name mentioned on a few French websites but could never really find a lot of information. His name was always revered and spoken in hushed tones. Gui became a mythical character in my search for the real Provence. Here is a slow cooked lamb stew largely inspired by him. . . . .

Herbal Rosé Infusion

1 bunch rosemary
1 bunch thyme
4 bay leaves
10 juniper berries
10 black peppercorns
4" segment of dried orange peel
1 bottle Rosé

Lamb Stew

¼ cup olive oil
10 thin carrots, peeled and sliced
1 sweet onion, peeled and sliced
2 ribs of celery, diced
1 leek, cleaned and diced
10 cloves garlic, sliced 'good fellas' thin
3 pounds boneless lamb shoulder,
   cut into 1-inch dices
2 teaspoons piment d'ville
2 teaspoons herbes de Provence
sea salt and black pepper to taste
2 tablespoons lavender honey
1 teaspoon freshly grated nutmeg

Chef's note: The easiest way to get freshly grated nutmeg is to use a microplane and do it yourself. The fresh scent will stand out.

Herbal Rosé Infusion

Bring eight quarts of water to a boil with the rosemary, thyme, bay leaves, juniper berries, black peppercorns and dried orange peel. Simmer 15 minutes then add bottle of Rosé. Continue simmering till the infusion has reduced by fifty percent. Strain out herbs and save liquid for making the lamb stew.

Lamb Stew

Sauté carrots, sweet onion, celery, leeks and garlic in olive oil. Cook five to ten minutes, or until the vegetables are soft.

While vegetables are cooking, season lamb shoulder with piment d'ville, herbes de Provence, sea salt, pepper and lavender honey. Sauté in oil over high heat until browned, about seven minutes. Add to vegetables, cover with Herbal Rosé Infusion and season with nutmeg.

Bring to a boil, then reduce to a simmer and cook covered till tender, about 2 - 3 hours. Serve the stew in large warmed bowls with mashed potatoes, roast potatoes, rice or nothing at all.

Dried Oranges

Dried oranges are a common element used in Provençal cooking. They are so easily made it almost embarrasses me to think I used to buy them. Simply peel an orange and hang it to dry in a breezy, cool and dry place for five days, or until fully dry. Lends an intense, concentrated orange flavor to everything it is cooked with.

Côte de Boeuf
Tomato Confit, Garlicky Swiss Chard

Côte de boeuf is a bone-in rib eye usually big enough for two. In 2014, I was a contestant on 'Guy's Grocery Games', a wildly popular show on the Food Network hosted by Guy Fieri. One challenge was to make a typical Sunday lunch for your family. I had been on a big steak kick and was entranced with wet-aged bone-in rib eyes. I fluctuated between an Italian bisteeca Fiorentina and the French version, côte de boeuf with Béarnaise. When I presented my côte de boeuf to the judges they told me no one ate like that at home. Then they asked if they could come over some Sunday. I don't eat beef often but when I do this is what we eat. . . . .

Steaks
2 - 36 ounce bone-in rib eye steaks
1 tablespoon flaky sea salt
2 teaspoons coarse black pepper
2 teaspoons piment d'ville
1 tablespoon chopped thyme
1 tablespoon chopped rosemary
1 tablespoon chopped oregano
8 garlic cloves, chopped
1/4 cup olive oil
2 tablespoons porcini powder, optional

Swiss Chard
1 bunch Swiss chard, any color
1 tablespoon olive oil
1 teaspoon red chili flakes
8 cloves garlic, sliced thin
salt and black pepper
1 tablespoon unsalted butter

Plating the Dish
2 tablespoons fruity olive oil
flaky smoked sea salt
1 recipe tomato confit, see page 73

Steaks
Pull the steaks out of the refrigerator and let sit for two hours at room temperature. Build a big fire in your charcoal grill. While you are waiting for the coals to be ready, season steaks with salt, pepper, piment d'ville, thyme, rosemary, oregano, garlic and a 1/4 cup of olive oil. If you want to add a beautiful earthy flavor, sprinkle porcini powder over as well. Cook steaks over white hot coals to your desired temperature. Let meat rest ten minutes before cutting.

Swiss Chard
Remove stems from the leaves and rough chop each separately. Drop stems in rapidly boiling salted water and let cook for two minutes before adding leaves. Continue cooking till leaves are tender, about five minutes. Cool off under cold running water then pat dry.

Put olive oil, chili flakes and garlic in a cold saute pan. Turn on heat, and cook till garlic starts getting a light amber color, a few minutes. Add Swiss chard and cook till warmed throughout. Season with salt and pepper. Finish with a big knob of butter. Put into a serving dish.

Plating the Dish
Cut bone off and lay on a warmed serving platter. Slice the meat thinly and reassemble steak on serving platter next to bone. Drizzle with fruity olive oil and sprinkle with flaky smoked sea salt. Serve Swiss chard and tomato confit on side.

"I LOVE TO PICK TOMATOES AT THE END OF THE
DAY, WHEN THEY'RE STILL WARM FROM THE SUN."
– ALAIN DUCASSE

Tomato Confit
Slow Roasted Tomatoes

Tomato confit are a foundation element in my cooking. I love the way the tomato flavors intensify and sweeten after long, slow cooking. They marry beautifully with almost everything, from lamb, chicken, fish to pastas and goat cheeses. As a consequence they find their way into a lot of my dishes. I use the same technique for all tomatoes, whether they are sweet cherry tomatoes or the meatier Romas. I modified my method drastically after spending a few months visiting my good friend Peter in New York and tasting his version. He conceived it after a trip to Puerto Rico where powdered onions and garlic infused their palate. Yes, gasp, if you are anything like me you are muttering 'powdered vegetables to season food'?! . . . .

6 Roma tomatoes
or 6 tomatoes on the vine
or 1 container of cherry tomatoes
1/4 cup olive oil
2 teaspoons herbes de Provence
1 teaspoon onion powder
1 teaspoon garlic powder
2 teaspoons sea salt
1/2 teaspoon black pepper
1 sprig thyme
1 bay leaf

Whole Tomato Version
Preheat your oven to 325 degrees. Put tomatoes into a saute pan. Pour olive oil over. Season with herbes de Provence, onion powder, garlic powder, sea salt and black pepper. Add both the thyme and bay leaf and bake for two hours. The tomatoes will look wrinkled, blistered and slightly reduced.

Sliced Tomato Version
Preheat your oven to 300 degrees. Slice the tomatoes quarter of an inch and lay on a silpat covered sheet pan. Drizzle olive oil over. Season with herbes de Provence, onion powder, garlic powder, sea salt and black pepper. Add both the thyme and bay leaf and bake for two hours. The tomatoes will have shrunken somewhat and lost a lot of moisture.

Beef Cheek Daube

Slow Cooked Beef, Olive and Orange Stew, Saffron Risotto

Maybe I am one of Pavlov's dogs. I start craving beef daube as soon as the cool Fall weather starts. It probably corresponds to a single moment when my wife Lisa and I lived in a small, off the grid hippie cabin deep in the woods of Mendocino, California. Fall had started in earnest and we decided to go for a long walk foraging for wild cèpes (porcini). I built a huge fire in our wood burning stove and placed a daube of beef to slow cook on top. We opened a bottle of wine to decant and walked out into the cool, misty day heady with pine scents. After walking two miles, we had collected two full shopping bags of mushrooms and headed back home to enjoy our simple feast. The closer to the cabin we got, the hungrier we became. The wood smoke and rich beef scents hung in the mist surrounding the cabin, enticing us to come in and eat. We started with cèpes persillade, a family favorite of cèpes cooked over a wood fire in duck fat with copious quantities of garlic and parsley, then tucked into the beef daube, followed by a green salad and local goat cheese. I was in foodie nirvana. . . . .

Marinating the Beef Cheeks

4 beef cheeks, trimmed of excess fat
1 orange, zested and juiced
1 cinnamon stick
1 whole star anise
2 cups big red wine

Making the Daube

¼ cup olive oil
3 medium carrots, sliced
1 sweet onion, large dice
¼ cup mashed garlic
4 ounces slab bacon, diced
1 tablespoon flour
14 ounces San Marzano tomatoes
1 cup chicken or veal stock
big pinch saffron
6 anchovy fillets, chopped
1 cup Picholine Olives

Marinating the Beef Cheeks

Marinate trimmed beef cheeks in orange juice and zest, cinnamon, star anise and red wine overnight. Strain marinade, reserving both the liquid and meat.

Making the Daube

Pat cheeks dry and sauté in olive oil till browned, about five minutes. Remove from pan and reserve. Add carrots and onion to pan and sauté till softened, about five minutes. Add garlic and bacon and cook till fragrant. Sprinkle with flour. Add tomatoes, stock and beef cheek marinade. Stir well to incorporate everything. Add remaining ingredients and simmer slow for five hours, or until beef is tender.

Saffron Risotto

1 tablespoon olive oil
1/2 cup sweet onion, diced fine
1 cup carnaroli rice
1 big pinch saffron
1/2 cup white wine
4 cups chicken stock
sea salt and black pepper
2 tablespoons unsalted butter
1 cup grated Reggiano Parmesan

To Plate

fruity French Olive Oil
2 tablespoons chopped parsley

Saffron Risotto

Heat oil in a non-reactive pan, add chopped onions and cook over medium heat till soft and translucent. Add the rice and saffron and stir with a wooden spoon for a few minutes. Turn the heat to high and add white wine and two cups of stock. Bring to a boil, then reduce back to low to medium heat and keep stirring. The rice takes about 30 minutes to cook. You need to stir often to help release starch from the rice which gives risotto its characteristic creamy texture. Keep adding small amounts of stock to keep rice moist. The rice should still have a slight bite and not be mushy. The consistency should be moist but not runny. Season with sea salt and pepper then rapidly stir in both butter and grated Parmesan.

To Plate

Put a quarter of the saffron risotto in the center of a warm plate. Top with one beef cheek and a drizzle of French olive oil. Sprinkle with chopped parsley. Enjoy with a hearty Provençal red wine like Domaine de Trevallon.

Beef Daube Cannelloni

Slow Cooked Beef, Olive and Swiss Chard, whatever Cheese you have

Provence was a poor region spawning a very frugal diet. No food is ever thrown away or wasted. Instead, leftovers are recycled and given a breath of new life. This dish is the prime example of taking a small amount of leftovers and turning it into another substantial meal. A lot of people are often curious about the Italian influence in Provençal food. The area around Nice was once part of the Italian Kingdom of Savoy. It traded hands a few times before permanently becoming part of France in 1860. I think a lot more had to do with its location. The combination of its proximity to Italy and isolation resulted in a cuisine of its own. Large parts of Provence were cut off from the mainland of France by the rugged terrain. The coast did not really open up till the event of railroads. This allowed the Provençal coast to develop their own independent cuisine and culture. . . . .

Pasta Sheets
pasta dough, see page 86

Beef Daube Filling
1 tablespoon olive oil
1 small sweet onion, sliced
4 leaves Swiss chard
2 beef cheeks, from daube page 74
sea salt and black pepper

Sauce and Finishing the Dish
1 cup daube sauce
1 cup chicken stock
sea salt and black pepper
1/4 cup grated Gruyère cheese or
whatever cheese you have

Pasta Sheets
Roll dough out to the same thickness as described on page 86. Cut pasta sheets into 8 - four inch lengths. Cook in rapidly boiling salted water for thirty seconds. Immediately plunge into a big bowl of ice water to prevent overcooking. Drain cooked sheets and pat dry. Reserve till you are ready to fill cannellonis.

Beef Daube Filling
Sauté sliced onion in olive oil till lightly browned and soft. Chop Swiss chard stems and add to onions. Continue cooking for two minutes then remove from heat.

Blanch Swiss chard leaves in rapidly boiling leftover pasta water. Drain and chop very coarsely. Add leaves to cooking onions and stems. Rough chop beefs cheeks and add. Salt and pepper to taste.

Sauce and Finishing the Dish
Heat leftover daube sauce along with chicken stock. Season with salt and pepper, if needed. Lay eight pasta sheets out on your counter. Divide filling into eight portions. Put filling on pasta sheet and roll tightly. Lay cannellonis in a oven proof serving dish drizzled with olive oil. Pour sauce over and sprinkle with grated cheese. Bake in a 400 degree oven for ten minutes, or until hot and bubbly. Serve with a beautiful green salad.

Roast Tail and Trotters Secreto

Wild Arugula, New Haven Peaches, Mustard Vinaigrette

A simple, refreshing summertime combination of succulent roast pork and tree ripened peaches. This dish got its foundation while spit roasting macadamia finished pork over an almond wood fire during the intense summer heat in Southern California. The dish reminds me of something my mother would prepare for us with leftover roasted pork loin, some salad and juicy stone fruits. . . . .

Mustard Vinaigrette

2 tablespoons red wine vinegar
1/4 cup stone ground mustard
sea salt and black pepper
1 cup olive oil, NOT extra virgin

Roasting the Pork

16 ounces secreto pork
1 tablespoon flaky sea salt
1 tablespoon piment d'ville
1 tablespoon herbes de Provence

Finishing the Dish

2 ounces baby wild arugula
2 New Haven peaches, sliced*
2 ounces shaved Parmesan

Substitute a different great peach perfectly in season or even another stone fruit like plums or nectarines.

Mustard Vinaigrette

Whisk together the red wine vinegar, stone ground mustard, sea salt and black pepper. Slowly whisk in the olive oil. If the dressing is too thick whisk in a bit of hot water to thin. Taste and adjust seasonings.

Roasting the Pork

Season secreto with sea salt flakes, piment d'ville and herbes de Provence. Sear in a hot pan, making sure both sides are nicely browned. Finish in a 350 degree oven for one hour. If you remember, flip it over half way in the cooking process. Chill roast pork.

Finishing the Dish

Arrange thinly sliced pork on a chilled plate, top with baby arugula, peaches and shaved Parmesan. Drizzle with mustard vinaigrette and serve.

Chef's Note: So what the hell is the secreto anyway?
Ask ten butchers and you will get ten different answers, maybe eleven. If you search the Internet you will be confounded with even more answers varying from Wikipedia's straightforward "It is the pork equivalent of the skirt steak" to James Peisker's answer in a fantastic Chicago Tribune article entitled 'The Secret of Secreto' in which he was quoted as saying "Completely different parts. A guy from Argentina told us it was the culotte off of pork chops — the cap. So if you have your pork chop section? Imagine it as a rib eye and (waving his hands) you have a rib eye cap. You have the same muscle in the pigs," Peisker said, disillusioning me a little more with each word. "Chris went to Curate (in Asheville, N.C.) and they were serving 'secreto' and it was the inner skirt steak. And then (noted Detroit chef and 'Charcuterie' co-author) Brian Polcyn in a demonstration said that it was the top blade steak, which we call the paleron." Tails and Trotters lists it as pork brisket and since I bought it from them I will stick to that. Secreto is a hard cut to find but worthy of the effort. It has a beautiful flavor and is a perfect meat for slow cooking.

"A COOK IS CREATIVE, MARRYING
INGREDIENTS IN THE WAY A POET
MARRIES WORDS."
— ROGER VERGE

Panisses

Chickpea Frites , Herbes de Provence and Piment d'Ville

Panisses have gained a lot of popularity since I first started cooking them in restaurants over 15 years ago. Cooking panisses is a lot like the process of making fried polenta. You start by making a thick porridge, cool it off, then fry various shapes. Panisses are so yummy to eat, are gluten free and will help you develop great arm muscles if you make them often. Panisses make a wonderful accompaniment to roast chickens, lamb and stews but are best eaten alone. Make a rich dipping sauce like rouille or a spicy harissa flavored aioli to kick it up a notch. . . . .

Chickpea Frites
2 cups chickpea flour
4 cups water
1 teaspoon sea salt
1/4 teaspoon black pepper
2 teaspoons cumin
1 teaspoon herbes de Provence
1 teaspoon piment d'ville

To Finish
10 cups peanut oil, for frying
2 ounces Parmesan, grated
1 tablespoon chopped parsley

Chef's Note: *Experiment with the flavors. Try adding chopped olives and sun dried tomatoes to the panisse mixture. Try different spice combinations. Let your imagination be your guide.*

Chickpea Frites

Whisk chickpea flour, water, sea salt, black pepper, cumin, herbes de Provence and piment d'ville together thoroughly.

Cook mixture on moderate heat in a heavy bottomed pan constantly stirring to prevent lumps. After cooking for four minutes the mixture will start to thicken to the consistency of a pancake batter. Keep stirring away. By six minutes the mixture is thick and spurting like a mini volcano. Keep stirring and dodge panisse lava shooting in the air. After ten minutes it will be very thick and prone to scorching the bottom. Continue cooking, stirring even more furiously till mixture is super thick and bubbling like a volcano, about 20 minutes in total. Immediately pour onto a pre-oiled baking sheet. Oil the bottom of another sheet and place on top gently pressing down. The panisse mixture should be about 1/2 inch thick. If you want rustic panisses just pour mixture on oiled dinner plates. The shapes will be less precise but equally delicious.

To Finish
Refrigerate for a few hours or overnight. Cut into finger shaped fries and deep fry at 350 degrees till brown and crispy, about five minutes. Toss in a bowl with Parmesan and parsley and eat right away!

Harissa Aioli
Harissa Aioli is quickly made by mixing 1/2 cup of mayonnaise with as much harissa paste or powder as you like. Adjust seasonings with a touch of sea salt. Or use rouille as a dipping sauce, see page 39.

DeNoble Farms
Sustainable Farm Fresh Produce Locally Grown in Tillamook, Oregon

Anyone who knows me well knows about my infatuation with artichokes. During their long season, I eat them at least four times a week in many different guises. Sometimes they appear on my lunch table as artichoke tarte Tatin, sometimes as artichokes barigoule. Lately I have been par-boiling them then charring on a hot grill and serving slathered in pesto with a ball of homemade burrata.

The only person who surpasses my lust for them may have been the late, great Catherine de Medici. She arrived at the French Court in 1533 at the tender age of 14 to marry King Henry II. Depending on the history theory you subscribe to, she either introduced or re-introduced artichokes to France. Regardless, she apparently ate so many that court chroniclers thought she would likely explode from the sheer volume of her indulgences. Artichokes were considered a powerful aphrodisiac. She shocked an elderly woman of the Court who prudently wrote "If one of us had eaten artichokes, we would have been pointed out in the street. Today young women are more forward than pages at the court." I have no one left to offend so I eat them with reckless abandon.

DeNoble Farms is a sustainably run family farm located on the Oregon Coast in Tillamook, the cheese capitol of Oregon, owned and operated by Tom and Patreece DeNoble and their children. They started farming in 1996 when they were growing specialty cut flowers for the wholesale market. They switched to growing artichokes sustainably in 2001 using natural growing practices, such as applying organic compost & fertilizers, doing crop rotations, use of beneficial insects, and only using organic sprays when absolutely necessary.

Each year the DeNobles grow more and more vegetable varieties. In 2009, they bought a larger farm and decided to put all their focus on growing fresh produce for the farmers markets and restaurants in Oregon. "We have seen tremendous growth over the last six years. The demand for quality fresh produce just keeps expanding," explains Patreece. "We have two children that work with us on the farm. Our daughter, Lexi, 22, and our son, Chandler, 19. They literally have grown up at the farmer's markets and both played integral parts in expanding our restaurant accounts throughout the Portland area.

Patrice DeNoble

We are best known for our Concerto and Opera artichokes - Italian heirloom varieties. They do really well in our coastal climate. The moderate temperatures and rich fertile soils produce very high quality vegetables that are huge and delicious. We are able to grow produce year round by using greenhouses and planting over wintering crop varieties. We haven't had our farm certified, but we do grow everything organically."

Artichokes Barigoule

Baby Artichokes simmered in White Wine, Thyme and Basil

Artichokes barigoule have always held a special place in my heart and stomach. The mere mention conjures golden sunlit landscapes of Provence in my head. It's so vivid that I can actually smell Provence in my mind. There were two dishes my mother held in reverence, a true civet de lapin, or rabbit stew thickened with the blood of the rabbit, and artichokes barigoule. These encapsulated her fondest food memories. My version of barigoule is more of a restaurant version made more luxuriously finished with sweet cream butter. I started adding butter when I turned it into a sauce for grilled loup de mer. Now I do all the time. . . . .

Cooking Artichokes

1 pound baby artichokes, about 10 to 12

1 lemon, sliced thin

1 tablespoon sea salt

2 quarts water

To Finish

1 cup of artichoke cooking liquid

1 cup white wine

1/4 cup fruity olive oil

3 ounces smoked lamb bacon, diced

2 young carrots, peeled and sliced

3 cloves spring garlic, mashed

2 thyme sprigs

1 bay leaf

1 lemon, zest and juice

1/4 cup basil, sliced

2 ounces unsalted butter, optional

sea salt and black pepper

Cooking Artichokes

Trim the top and bottom 1/4 inch off the baby artichokes. Use a sharp paring knife and trim the outer leaves off. Peel the stem if there is one attached. Cut the artichoke in half lengthwise and drop into a pot with the lemon, sea salt and water. Bring to a boil, then simmer till tender, about 20 minutes. The tip of a knife should easily pierce the artichoke.

To Finish

Put one cup artichoke cooking liquid, white wine and olive oil in a pan and bring to a boil. Add lamb bacon, carrots, garlic, thyme and bay leaf. Simmer till carrots are tender, about 15 minutes. Add artichokes, lemon zest and some lemon juice. I say some lemon juice because I want you to taste it. Add just enough to taste it slightly. The purpose is to add just enough bright acidity to cut the fattiness of the olive oil and butter. The lemon flavor should not overpower the barigoule. Add basil and whisk in butter. Adjust salt and pepper and serve.

Spring Artichokes

The joy of Spring Artichokes. The best artichokes of the season come from early Spring long before the choke is able to form. Don't let this discourage you from seeking out and finding them. I buy my artichokes exclusively from DeNoble Farms in Tillamook. Their season extends till November.

Artichoke & Goat Cheese Ravioli

Tomato Confit, baby Arugula, Barigoule Jus

My absolute greatest joy in life is cooking with my four year old son Beaumont. Children have such a simple, practical approach to tackling problems. Their playful nature and ability to laugh at themselves is the perfect foil to feeling stressed in a kitchen. Food should be fun to make. The emotion put into a dish is translated to the experience eating it. This ravioli is born out of the frugality of the French. We never have leftovers; only new dishes waiting to be discovered. . . . .

Egg Pasta
2 whole eggs
2 egg yolks
1 tablespoon water
1 teaspoon sea salt
10 ounces all purpose flour
1 egg, beaten

Filling
1 cup leftover artichokes barigoule, page 85
4 ounces fresh goat cheese
1 tablespoon fresh basil, chopped

Garnishes
1/2 cup barigoule juices
2 tablespoons unsalted butter
1 cup cherry tomato confit, see page 73
1 ounce baby arugula
thinly shaved Parmesan
1 to 2 tablespoons French Olive Oil

Egg Pasta
Whisk together the whole eggs, egg yolks, water and salt. Put the flour in a stand mixer armed with the hook attachment. With the motor running on low speed, slowly add the egg mixture to the flour and knead for eight minutes. You will occasionally have to stop the mixer and gather everything into a ball then resume. Put the pasta dough into a zip lock bag, squeeze out air and let pasta rest at least one hour, better one day. As the pasta rests, it fully hydrates the flour making a better dough. Prior to reading Paul Bertolli's book 'Cooking by Hand', I really screwed up pasta dough.

Filling
Pulse the artichokes barigoule in your food processor till coarse. Add the goat cheese and basil and mix thoroughly by hand. Fill a pastry bag or even a gallon zip lock with a corner cut out. Now you are ready to make raviolis.

Crafting the ravioli
Cut the dough into four equal sized pieces. Use a pasta machine to roll your dough into four long sheets. I bought mine at a budget store for $6. Most pasta machines have a series of numbers on a dial that correspond to the space between the two rollers. Start at the widest setting and continue rolling each sheet through every number till you reach the second to last number. If the dough starts to stick, sprinkle a small amount of flour over. Lay the sheet on a lightly floured surface and brush with a beaten egg. This will seal the dough together when you fold the sheet over. Pipe 10 teaspoon sized mounds of filling every 1.5 inches like the picture to the right. Fold the dough over, pressing inbetween each mound removing air bubbles and sealing the sides. Use a ravioli cutter or a sharp knife to separate into individual ravioli. Repeat with remaining dough and filling.

Finishing the dish
Bring a pot of salted water to a rapid boil. Drop each ravioli into the water and cook three minutes. Fresh pasta cooks way quicker than dried. In the meantime bring the barigoule juices to a boil with the butter. Use a slotted spoon to remove the raviolis from water and drop straight into the sauce. Toss in the cherry tomato confit. Spoon raviolis onto a platter. Scatter arugula over and top with shaved Parmesan. Drizzle French olive oil over and enjoy!

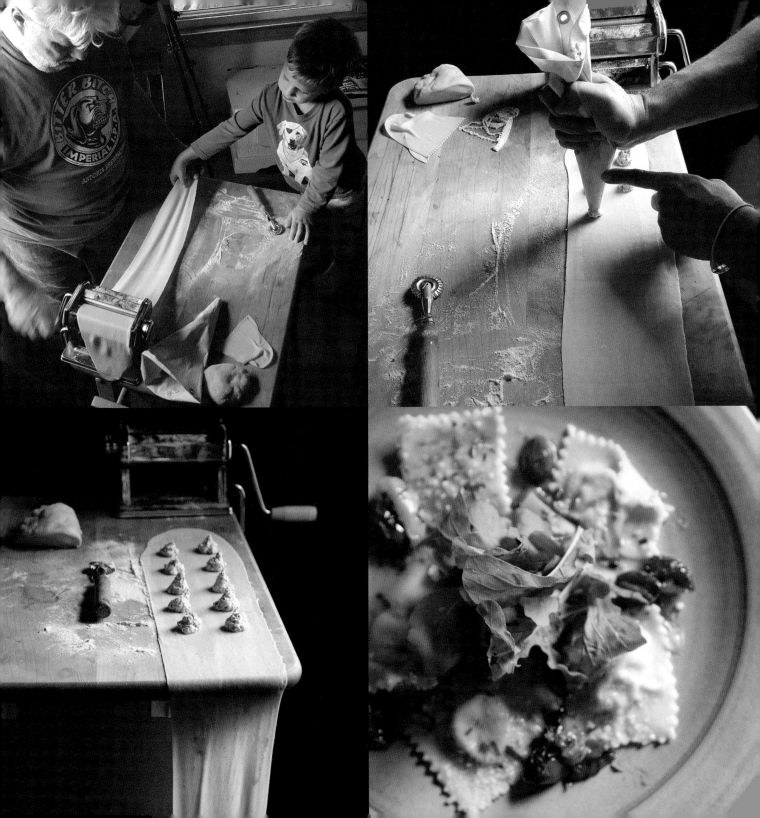

Eggplant
$2.50
/Lb

Ratatouille
Provençal Vegetable Stew

When I was a small child my mother used to keep a jar of ratatouille in the refrigerator at all times. It scared me to death. For some reason, I thought eggplant was a plant made from chicken eggs. It disgusted me. My mother would eat it by the bowl load; cold, hot it didn't matter. I could never fathom her love for it. Now it is something I keep on hand during the summer months when all the ingredients are at their peak flavors. It's fantastic with poached eggs served on top, rolled into a creamy omelet or just eaten alone. Ratatouille will go well with whatever you are serving, from roast chicken to grilled lamb chops to a simple piece of fish. Try burning the skins off the pepper to introduce a smoky aspect like Richard Olney describes in 'Lulu's Provençal Table'.

I have made ratatouille a bunch of different ways over the course of my career but now have settled on this method. I used to cut each ingredient into a very small dice and sauté separately, combining only in the end. Visually and texturally each micro piece was its own entity. It photographed well. I thought I was at the height of my game as a Chef. My mother would rightfully complain that it was a restaurant version and not as good as the ones made at home. I used to fight her insisting as a Chef I knew better. Mother knows best. Now I agree with her. This is the longer cooked maman version. Do not be scared to add ingredients like green beans or even potatoes and olives. . . . .

Serves 8

2 Japanese eggplant, diced
1/2 cup olive oil
1 sweet onion, diced
2 red peppers, diced
3 zucchini, diced
4 cloves garlic, mashed
4 tomatoes, skinned, chopped
1 cup basil
sea salt and black pepper

To Finish
1 tablespoon French olive oil

Submerge the diced eggplant in ice cold water and let sit for ten minutes to remove any bitterness. I started soaking eggplant rather than salting after reading a cookbook of Japanese dishes. I found it works better.

Heat olive oil in a large pan and sauté onions and peppers together over low to medium heat till softened and translucent, about ten minutes. Drain eggplants well and add to onions and peppers. Continue cooking for another ten to fifteen minutes. The eggplant won't be fully cooked but will be on the way. Add zucchini, garlic and tomatoes and continue cooking on low heat till tender, about thirty minutes. Add basil, salt and pepper and cook five more minutes.

To Finish
Drizzle with a fruity French olive oil and enjoy!

Penne with Ratatouille
Tomato Sauce and Pistou

I grew up eating a lot of pasta. My family had many Italian friends and I suspect this is their influence on my palate. I love the simplicity of this pasta dish. It's perfect for when you want something simple and nourishing. I make large batches of tomato sauce and keep frozen for when I want something quick and easy. . . . .

Tomato Sauce

1/4 cup olive oil
1 sweet onion, chopped
2 cloves garlic, mashed
28 ounce can whole peeled San
   Marzano tomatoes
½ cup chopped basil leaves
pinch sugar
salt and pepper, to taste

Finishing the Pasta

1 tablespoon olive oil
2 cloves garlic, thinly sliced
1 teaspoon red pepper flakes
1 - 2 cups tomato sauce
2 cups ratatouille, see page 89
1 pound fresh Penne, cooked
sea salt and pepper, to taste
1 tablespoon French olive oil
grated Reggiano Parmesan
1 cup pistou, see page 18

Tomato Sauce

Sauté onion and garlic in olive oil till softened and translucent but with no color. Hand crush San Marzano tomatoes and add to onions.

Add everything else and let simmer for thirty minutes. Puree everything through a food mill. If you do not have one then put in a blender and pulse on low speed, You want it to be smooth but not pureed completely. The problem with blenders is they aerate things. Aeration will give it an orange creamy color and change the mouth feel.

Finishing the Pasta

I must have Sardinian blood in me somehow. So many things I cook begin the same way, reminiscent of the flavors there. Put olive oil, sliced garlic and red pepper flakes into a cold pan. Turn heat on and cook slowly till the garlic turns amber without burning. Add tomato sauce and ratatouille. I like my pasta with less sauce. Some like it very saucy. Use whatever amount you like. Add cooked penne and toss over low heat. Let pasta sit one minute soaking up the sauce. Adjust the salt and pepper. Drizzle with a fruity French olive oil and enjoy! Serve pistou and Parmesan on the side.

Simmering tomato sauce

Garlic and red pepper flakes in olive oil

Slow Roasted Tomatoes

Shepherd Vegetables
Charcoal Grilled Vegetables

I am not sure the exact origins of this recipe. I found it while researching the menu for my Provençal restaurant, Pili Pili. Perhaps I read it in one of Daudet's short stories. It was based on a simple vegetable preparation shepherds would make while tending flocks in the arid countryside of Provence. They would make a fire for dinner and put the vegetables to cook in the smoldering coals. Wild herbs gathered would be added to the vegetables. I love the simple elegance of this dish. It goes well with grilled lamb and seafood. . . . .

2 or 3 small, thin eggplants, cut in
   half, lengthwise
1 sweet onion, cut into wedges
3 red peppers, burn skin off than cut
   in fat juliennes
3 baby zucchini, cut in half, lengthwise
1 head garlic, cut in half separating
   top and bottom
16 cherry tomatoes, cooked confit,
   see page 73
1/4 cup olive oil
sea salt and black pepper, to taste
1 tablespoon herbes de Provence
1 tablespoon French olive oil

There are a few different ways to make this dish. The basic premise is to fully cook all the vegetables and flavor simply with herbs and olive oil. The closest to the original way shepherds would cook it is to grill everything over a charcoal fire then toss in olive oil and herbes de Provence. The charcoal lends a beautiful smoky accent oven roasting can't. I was roasting a chicken and simply threw the vegetables on the roasting pan under the chicken. While it isn't authentic it does manage to capture the spirit.

Mix all the vegetables in a bowl. Toss everything in olive oil, salt, pepper and herbes de Provence. Roast or grill to fully cooked and tender. Put into a serving dish and drizzle over a fruity finishing olive oil.

"I was guarding the flocks on Luberon Mountain, sometimes I remained whole weeks without seeing a living soul, alone with my dog and my sheep. Occasionally the hermit of the mountains passed by, hunting for herbs, or perchance I saw the black face of a Piedmont charcoal-burner; but these were simple men, silent through force of habit, men who had lost the liking for speech and who knew nothing of what went on down in the villages and towns."

- Alphonse Daudet, 'The Stars, The Tale of a Provençal Shepherd'

Pine Mushrooms Persillade

Duck Fat, Crunchy Garlic, and Parsley

Cèpes persillade is another near mythical dish in my family. Over the years phone conversations with my mother always centered around food. Eventually every call got to the point of discussing the joys of eating food, like cèpes persillade and the merits of a true rabbit civet properly thickened with fresh rabbit blood. Cèpes are more commonly known in America as porcinis. They can easily be found in markets in the Northwest. Our local farmer's market has them during the Spring and Fall flushes. I like using another popular Pacific Northwest mushroom called matsutakes, or pine mushrooms. The texture is incredibly similar to porcinis and the flavor is reminiscent of pine needles. Any wild or cultivated mushroom will work in this preparation.

It is strange how we organize memories in our head, especially when they were formed as a child. I remember touring Oradour-sur-Glane when I was very little. It is the remains of a French town horribly frozen in time from a World War II massacre in 1944. Nazi soldiers entered the town and methodically butchered all the citizens, including several hundreds of women and children burned in a small church. I vividly remember touring the village and feeling the heavy weight of blackness engulf me. I was curious, but desperately wanted to leave. Afterwards, we walked into nearby woods where I instantly felt freed from the terror. I felt as though I had escaped like very few of the towns people had a few decades before. We collected mushrooms as we walked. Somewhere in my child's memory is eating cèpes persillade and feeling joyous to be alive. . . . .

2 pounds wild matsutake mush-
    rooms, #1 petites if possible
1/4 cup duck fat or olive oil
8 fat garlic cloves, sliced thin
1/4 cup chopped parsley
sea salt and black pepper, to taste

Trim the bottoms of the matsutakes. Put them in a large bowl of cold water and let soak for five minutes. The mushrooms are very dense and will not soak up water. Periodically agitate the water to help dislodge the dirt. Use a slotted spoon to remove the mushrooms. Slice lengthwise.

In a large saute pan heat the duck fat and garlic over medium heat. Keep stirring to ensure even cooking. When garlic is amber colored remove with a slotted spoon and reserve. Sauté sliced mushrooms over high heat till lightly browned. Add the garlic and parsley and continue cooking for a few minutes. Season with sea salt and black pepper.

"Good food is the foundation of genuine happiness."
– Auguste Escoffier

Salted Caramel Apple Beignet
Salted Caramel Sauce

My family loves to go camping near Mount Hood in Oregon. One cold morning last Fall we woke up and didn't want to rush back home so we opted for a scenic drive down to the Columbia Gorge. On the way, we drove a scenic rural route winding through small towns dotted with picturesque apple and pear orchards called the Fruit Loop. Fall's arrival was heralded by crisp air and beautiful colored hues poking through the pine forest mosaic. We stopped by Draper Girls Country Farm to buy some produce and fresh pressed pear cider. We sampled old heirloom apples sweeter and crisper than any I'd previously tried. The golden nectar ran down my chin and through my sticky fingers and reminded me of beignets my mother would make. These salted caramel apple beignets easily cross the cultural border between America and France. . . . .

Marinating Apples
4 apples, peeled, cored and cut
    into ½ inch thick slices
1 cup Calvados, or apple brandy
1 cup sugar

Beignet Batter
1.5 cups all purpose flour
½ teaspoon sea salt
1 tablespoon sugar
2 egg yolks
¼ cup vegetable oil
1/2 bottle hard cider
2 egg whites

Salted Caramel Sauce
2 cups sugar
1/2 cup water
1 cup heavy cream
1 -2 teaspoons flaky sea salt
4 ounces unsalted butter

Finishing the Beignets
2 quarts vegetable oil, for frying
powdered sugar
1 pint caramel ice cream

Marinating Apples
Marinate apple slices in Calvados and sugar for at least a few hours, or better yet overnight.

Beignet Batter
Mix flour, sea salt and sugar together. Mix egg yolks, oil and cider together. Add wet ingredients to dry ingredients. Whip egg whites to medium peaks and fold in.

Salted Caramel Sauce
Put sugar and water into a stainless pot and bring to a rapid boil. Cook till it starts turning an amber color. Now you need to really start paying attention. Caramel goes from amber to jet black fairly quickly. Be super careful of getting caramel on your skin. Sugar burns are among the worst. Hot sugar sticks to your skin and continues to burn. You want to cook caramel till it turns a deep brown and not a second longer. Immediately add the heavy cream and pull off the stove. The cold cream will splatter and pop as it hits the caramel. It may even harden the caramel. Do not worry, this is completely normal. When it's done splattering, return to the burner and boil once again. Add sea salt and butter.

Finishing the Beignets
Dip apple slices in the beignet batter and deep fry at 350 degrees till golden brown, about five minutes. Flip the slices as they cook so they brown evenly. Drain well on paper towels.

Dust with copious quantities of powdered sugar. Now is not the time to worry about calories or diets. Drizzle liberally with caramel sauce and top with a scoop of caramel ice cream. Paradise!

Vacherin of Strawberries

Tarragon Frozen Yogurt, Strawberry Lavender Soup

I forewarn you, this is a recipe that involves a certain amount of skill to make correctly. It certainly falls more comfortably in the professional category than household. This variation of vacherin is the love child of mine and Sarah Estle, my Pastry Chef in Connecticut. Sarah now has her own business making the most amazing wedding cakes you've ever seen or tasted in your life. This is the first dessert we collaborated on when I took over the kitchens at Copper Beech Inn. I wanted something that screamed Summer and was classic enough for our French brasserie menu. Super sweet strawberries were coming in at Scott's Farm. I returned to the kitchens with a flat. Sarah immediately thought to pair the tarragon yogurt with a strawberry sorbet. I added the strawberry soup and together we ended up with this masterpiece. It remains one of my favorite desserts when strawberries are their sweetest. . . . . .

Strawberry Sorbet

2 cups sugar
2 cups water
one quart strawberries
1 lemon, juiced
pinch sea salt

Tarragon scented Frozen Yogurt

4 sprigs tarragon, chopped
1 cup milk, warmed
1 cup heavy cream
3/4 cup sugar
4 egg yolks
2 cups whole milk yogurt
pinch of salt

Meringues

4 egg whites, room temperature
1 -1/2 c. powdered sugar

Strawberry Sorbet

Simple syrup is just sugar and water brought to a boil and cooled. Mix simple syrup, strawberries, lemon juice and salt. Puree in a blender on low speed. Freeze according to the instructions of your ice cream machine's manufacturer.

Tarragon scented Frozen Yogurt

Steep tarragon in warm milk and cream for an hour. Discard all the tarragon and bring milk back to a boil.

Whisk sugar and egg yolks together till frothy and lemon colored. Temper yolks and milk together by whisking in half of hot milk to the egg yolks, then temper back into the pot of milk. Keep stirring with a wood spoon over low heat till sauce consistency. Sauce consistency is one of those terms you learn early in your cooking career. Put a wooden spoon into the frozen yogurt base and pull it out. Run your finger through the base on the back. If it holds the tracks of your finger than it is sauce consistency. Whisk in yogurt and salt, then freeze according to the instructions of your ice cream machine's manufacturer.

Meringues

Making meringues can be very intimidating. Steady yourself with a glass of wine. Preheat the oven to 200 degrees. Beat egg whites at high speed on your stand mixer till medium peaks form. Add sugar and continue whisking at high speed until the meringue is stiff and shiny, about one minute.

Vacherin of Strawberries
Continued from page 98

Strawberry Tarragon Soup
1 cup sugar
1 cup water
1 quart strawberries
1 sprig tarragon, chopped
pinch sea salt
lemon juice

Finishing the dessert
four beautiful strawberries
four tarragon mini sprigs
powdered sugar

Line a baking sheet with parchment paper. Now here is the part where you will have to channel your inner MacGyver. The goal is to create a layered tower of three meringue disks sandwiched with one layer of tarragon frozen yogurt and another of the strawberry sorbet. In a restaurant I would use metal tubes about two inches in diameter and about three inches high. Another method, though less friendly with the health department, is pvc pipe cut into suitable sections. Go to your local hardware store and play stupid. Usually the staff will take pity on you and perfectly cut them into the correct sizes. Chefs are a resourceful bunch. The food has to be served despite any obstacle. In a sense we are the postmen of the culinary world. Snow or shine we have to deliver the food. Be like a Chef, get creative with whatever you have in your house. Trace the interior diameter of the tube you selected on a piece of parchment 12 times. You do not want to eat the ink or pencil you traced with so flip the parchment over so you can still see the circles but the ink is on the other side. Put a small plain tip in a pastry bag and pipe concentric circles of meringue. Bake at 200 degrees for two hours or until thoroughly dried out and crispy. Ideally you want to end up with meringues with no color. Sometimes I have dried them out all night long with the oven set as low as it will go.

Meringues have a notoriously short shelf life and lose their crunch in humid climates or weather quickly. Here's another tip the Health Department doesn't like. I collect the little bags of drying agents that come with electronics and some spices to keep them dry. I find a Tupperware container and tape a few packets on the inside of the lid, out of contact with food. The meringues keep dry and crispy for a few days.

Strawberry Tarragon Soup
Make a simple syrup with the sugar and water. Put cooled syrup in a blender with the strawberries and tarragon and puree on low speed. Season with a pinch of salt and a squeeze of lemon juice. Keep cold till ready to use.

Finishing the dessert
Fill pvc tubes with one meringue, tarragon frozen yogurt, meringue, strawberry sorbet and finally a last meringue. Let freeze overnight. Push vacherin out of tubes and arrange in the center of a chilled soup bowl. Dust top with powdered sugar and garnish with a strawberry and a small tarragon sprig. Pour strawberry soup around and serve immediately.

Maman's Apple Tart
Caramel Ice Cream, Salted Caramel Sauce

What could be more soothing and comforting than a warm apple tart made by your mother? My maman had a natural talent for making delicious tarts and would make them all the time growing up. My mother adored these little yellow plums, called mirabelles in France, almost as much as she loved apples. When I became a Chef, I developed a Mirabelle tarte tatin and served it for years as a tribute to my mother. I eventually switched back to my mother's favorite fruit, apples. This tarte Tatin is my tribute to my mother. . . . .

Tart Dough
100 grams all purpose flour
1 teaspoon sugar
1/8 teaspoon sea salt
1/2 teaspoon baking powder
50 grams unsalted butter,
cold and diced
enough cold water

For the Apples
4 to 6 granny smith apples
2 tablespoons unsalted butter
1/2 cup sugar
1 orange, zested
pinch of cinnamon

To Finish
powdered sugar
1/2 cup caramel sauce, see page 97
4 scoops caramel ice cream

Chef's Note: Nowadays all digital scales have the ability to switch between ounces and grams effortlessly. Grams are a far more accurate measurement than ounces for pastry making.

Tart Dough
Sift together flour, sugar, sea salt and baking powder. Form a mound and mix in butter. You want to mix with your fingers till it resembles coarse corn meal. Make a small hole in the center and add a 1/4 cup of cold water. Start mixing the dough gently with your fingertips. Keep adding cold water till you have a soft dough. It should be able to form a ball and not be sticky. It's ok to have small clumps of butter. The main concern is over beating. I always use the analogy of working out. The more you exercise the firmer your muscles become. When you stop and rest, your muscles become softer again. Gluten reacts the same way. The more you work the dough the tougher it will be. Let dough rest one hour or overnight.

For the Apples
Peel and core apples. Cut each apple into four equal sized wedges through the stem. Cut each quarter in half so you are left with eight equal sized pieces. Melt the butter and sugar together and cook till sugar starts to caramelize. Add apples and continue cooking until they start to brown and are well coated with caramel, five to seven minutes. Add orange zest and cinnamon. You can do all of this the day before.

Line four Teflon blini pans or one 10-inch saute pan with apple wedges. Roll dough out evenly to 1/8 inch thickness. Cut circles slightly larger than blini pans. Cover apples with dough and tuck around edges. Bake in a 400 degree oven till dough is lightly browned, about ten to fifteen minutes.

Invert onto room temperature plate and dust with powdered sugar. Spoon sauce around and top with a scoop of caramel ice cream. Serve immediately.

Compote of Cherries
Lemon Verbena Ice Cream, Lemon Puffs

This is my kind of dessert; simple, vibrant, colorful, seasonal and exploding with flavors. The cherries are macerated in star anise, cinnamon and rum complementing the verbena wonderfully. Lemon Verbena is an herb I always grow in my kitchen garden. Its versatility works well with chicken, pork, veal and desserts. I also make an incredible liqueur from it. . . . .

Marinated Cherries
1 cup sugar
1 cup water
1/2 cup dark rum
1 cinnamon stick
2 star anise
1 pound cherries, pitted

Lemon Verbena Ice Cream
1 cup lemon verbena leaves
2 cups whole milk, warmed
1 cup sugar
pinch of salt
8 egg yolks, room temperature
2 cups heavy cream

Lemon Puffs
1 lemon, juiced and zested
1/4 cup powdered sugar
1 package puff pastry
1 cup sugar

Final Assembly
powdered sugar

Marinated Cherries
Bring sugar and water to a boil for two minutes, then turn off. Add rum, cinnamon and star anise and cool. Add cherries and macerate overnight.

Lemon Verbena Ice Cream
Let lemon verbena leaves infuse in warm milk for a few hours. Strain leaves out and bring milk to a boil.

Whisk sugar, salt and egg yolks together until lemon colored and fluffy. Add half of milk slowly to yolks while stirring constantly. Pour mixture into remaining milk and cook over low heat, constantly stirring with a wooden spoon till sauce consistency. Sauce consistency is achieved when you can drag your finger through the ice cream base on the back of a wood spoon and a permanent track appears. Add heavy cream and freeze in your ice cream machine according to the manufacturers instructions.

Lemon Puffs
Mix together one tablespoon of lemon juice, lemon zest and powdered sugar and reserve.

Remove puff pastry from package, dredge in granulated sugar and roll till it is 1/8th inch thick. Cut into 1/8 inch wide by 6 inch long rectangles and freeze till firm. Brush with lemon sugar mixture and bake at 450 degrees on a silpat till lightly browned, about seven minutes. Brush again with lemon sugar mixture. Cool completely.

Final Assembly
Put a spoonful of the macerated cherries in the bottom of a chilled bowl. Top with a scoop of lemon verbena ice cream and two lemon puffs heavily sprinkled with powdered sugar.

Roasted Peaches

Brown Sugar and Vanilla Butter, Vanilla Ice Cream

Cherries may mark the beginning of Summer, but tree ripened peaches let you know it's here, for real. The farmer's market in Portland is flooded with beautiful peaches grown in Hood River, Oregon. This is the perfect dessert for when you want something quick, easy and simple enough that even a four year old with a plastic knife and a very short attention span can make.

Peaches have been eaten for 1,000's of years. They originated in China where they were enjoyed in an almost cult-like status. A steamed roll the shape of a peach is traditionally served on birthdays called shoutao, which translates to 'long life peach'. Peaches symbolized immortality. In 1977, researchers unearthed the well-preserved body of a woman buried in 200 BC with a bowl of peaches. Marco Polo reported finding peaches weighing a full two pounds each. Eventually they found their way to Europe where King Louis the XIV was an enthusiastic fan. He reportedly gave pension to a man who grew the best peaches just outside of Paris for him. Though Louis shared them with American Indians who were brought to France, it is believed that the Spaniards brought them to our shores. The Natchez Indians became such fervent fans that they even named one of their thirteen months after peaches.

This recipe is so simple it requires nothing more than a few words. It is a great last minute dessert when you want something sweet but do not feel like cooking. . . . .

Simply cut peaches in half and remove the pit. Top with a giant knob of grass-fed unsalted butter and sprinkle liberally with brown sugar. Arrange on a baking sheet and put in the broiler as close to flame as possible. Cook till the sugar caramelizes, about five minutes or so. Mix 1/4 cup of water and 1/4 cup of sugar in a small pan. Bring to a furious boil and add a vanilla bean split in two. Pour any juices saved from the broiled peaches into the vanilla syrup and use this as your sauce. Top with a spoonful of your favorite ice cream and enjoy the lingering tastes of Summer.

"Chocolate's okay, but I prefer a really intense fruit taste. You know when a peach is absolutely perfect... it's sublime. I'd like to capture that and then use it in a dessert."
— Kathy Mattea

Brown Butter and Fig Tart
Vanilla Bean Ice Cream

Everyone knows I am not much of a dessert eater. I prefer to finish a meal with a green salad and a plate of cheeses. Occasionally I encounter a dessert so delicious that I cannot resist. I first tasted a version of this tart at Pili Pili, my Provençal restaurant in Chicago, when my Pastry Chef made this for a special. I was struck by the simplicity. No Provençal maman would claim this dessert as original, but they would welcome it into their hearts. If you are feeling adventurous and have an ice cream maker, try making a goat cheese ice cream to accompany it. . . . .

Brown Butter Tart Filling
6 ounces unsalted butter
1 vanilla bean, cut in half lengthwise
3 eggs
1 cup sugar
4/5 cup flour
1 orange, zest only

Tart Dough
1 vanilla bean, seeds scraped out
3 tablespoons butter, room temp
1/2 cup powdered sugar
2 egg yolks
1 cup flour
1/4 teaspoon baking powder
pinch sea salt

To Finish
10 ripe figs, cut in half
1 tablespoon brown sugar
1/4 cup powdered sugar
1 quart vanilla bean ice cream

Chef's Note: Flour acts like a muscle when you make dough. The more you work the dough the stronger the muscle and the tougher it becomes. Resting dough acts the same way. The longer the dough rests, the more the gluten rests and the more tender it becomes.

Brown Butter Tart Filling
Brown butter and vanilla bean in a pan over medium heat, about five minutes. The flavor comes from the nuttiness of browned butter. Let butter cool slightly. Fish out vanilla pod and keep for a decoration. Whisk together eggs, sugar, flour and orange zest. Drizzle in brown butter. Reserve till you are ready to bake the tart.

Tart Dough
Put vanilla bean seeds, room temperature butter, sugar and egg yolks into the bowl of a food processor fitted with the steel blade. Process till smooth. Add flour, baking powder and sea salt. Process just long enough till it is well mixed. Knead into a ball, cover with plastic wrap and refrigerate for one hour.

To Finish
Remove dough from refrigerator. If it is rock hard, beat it with a tapered rolling pin till it is slightly malleable. Dust a surface with flour and roll dough out till you have an 1/8 inch thick rectangle slightly larger than your tart pan. Line a rectangle shaped tart pan (13X4X1) with dough. Crimp the edges, pinching hard. Allow dough to hang over messily. Let tart relax in your refrigerator for two hours. Line tart shell with aluminum foil and fill with baking beans (or raw rice). The heavy crimping and baking beans help keep dough from shrinking while cooking. Bake in a 400 degree preheated oven for ten minutes. Remove foil and cook another two minutes. Use your rolling pin to roll over the top of the tart shell breaking loose those unsightly edges.

Pour brown butter filling in. Lay the fig halves in a line down the center flesh side face up. Sprinkle brown sugar over them and bake at 400 degrees till brown. I did mine for 40 minutes. It is done when a toothpick comes out clean and the tart filling is firm but not hard. Every oven cooks differently and at different temperatures. Learn yours. You may find yourself turning the oven down lower halfway through cooking or maybe even turning the temperature up. The goal is a cooked tart that is not burnt. Sprinkle with powdered sugar and serve with a scoop of ice cream.

Chocolate Profiteroles

Turkish Coffee Ice Cream, Goat Milk Caramel, Hot Chocolate Sauce

OK, how far from the Mediterranean can we stray and still feel justified to include this bastion of French desserts in this book? Profiteroles are to desserts what the ubiquitous New England clam chowder is to soup. . . .

Pâte à choux
1 cup water
1 pinch sea salt
1 stick of unsalted butter (4 oz)
1 cup all purpose flour
4 eggs
1 egg beaten (for egg wash)

Chocolate sauce
2 cups water
1 cup heavy cream
9 ounces bittersweet Chocolate
¾ cup sugar
sea salt, to taste

Final Assembly of the dish
1 quart Turkish Coffee Ice Cream
   (or whatever flavor you like)
powdered sugar
1 jar goat milk caramel

Pâte à choux
Preheat oven to 425 degrees. Line a baking sheet with a silpat or buttered parchment paper. Place the water, sea salt and butter in a stainless steel pot and bring to a rapid boil. Using a wooden spoon stir in all the flour at once. Keep stirring till well incorporated and your arm is sore. Continue cooking till dough dries out slightly, about one minute.

Let rest five minutes to cool down then add eggs one at a time till well incorporated or if you are feeling lazy use your food processor.

Pipe little golf ball sized puffs with a plain tip. Brush with egg wash and bake at 400 degrees for 20 minutes. Turn oven down to 350 and bake for another 20 minutes.

Chocolate sauce
Mix all the sauce ingredients in a pot and bring to a boil. Simmer till it reduces down to sauce consistency. Season with a pinch of sea salt for extra flavor.

Final assembly of the dish
Cut profiteroles in half and fill with a scoop of ice cream. Arrange in a pyramid on a serving plate. Sprinkle with powdered sugar.

Drizzle with both chocolate sauce and goat caramel.

"French cooking is not complicated," I keep telling those who insist it is. At least it does not have to be. I think it is the foreign-sounding names of dishes that often strike terror in the hearts of innocent cooks."
— Julia Child

No one is born a great cook,
one learns by doing.
— Julia Child

Julia Child's Chocolate Cake

Lindt Salted Dark Chocolate and Almond Cake

As a child I was fascinated by Julia. I watched her shows from my mother's lap. Her lust for life and fearless approach to cooking captivated me. Later in life I came to fully appreciate her importance in developing the America's palate. Learning new things can be very intimidating, especially when you add complex sounding foreign words like soufflé. Julia broke the barriers down and made it possible for anyone to cook. She spoke at my cooking school graduation though sadly I did not attend, I was too busy cooking. I wish I had the opportunity to meet and thank her for the thumb-print she had on my career. . . . .

butter and flour to prepare cake pan
4 ounces Lindt dark chocolate with a
  touch of sea salt
2/3 cup sugar
4 ounces unsalted butter
3 egg yolks
3 egg whites
1 tablespoon sugar
1/2 cup sifted flour
1/3 cup almond meal
1 teaspoon vanilla extract

Chef's Note: *Almond meal is simply very finely ground almonds. It is hard to get the same results at home because you usually end up making almond butter. If you want to try, put toasted Marcona almonds in a food processor with a spoonful of sugar and process till super-fine. The sugar keeps the almonds from turning into butter.*

I grew up eating Lindt chocolate. Find the salted version in grocery stores everywhere.

Preheat oven to 350 degrees. Butter an 8 inch spring form cake pan. Dust with flour, shaking the excess out into a garbage can. Set aside.

Melt 4 ounces of chocolate over a gently simmering double boiler. When it is melted, remove from heat and let cool slightly.

Beat sugar and butter till pale yellow and fluffy in a stand mixer. Add egg yolks and reserve till needed.

Beat egg whites in a stand mixer till you have soft peaks of billowy white egg whites. It will look like a mound of snow. Add 1 tablespoon of sugar and continue beating at high speed for 30 seconds. The egg whites will start to look shiny and stiff peaks will appear.

With a rubber spatula, add melted chocolate to egg yolk mixture. Add flour, almond meal and vanilla. Gently fold in one third of beaten egg whites. Add remaining egg whites gently as to lighten the batter.

Spoon into your prepared spring form pan and bake at 350 degrees for 25 minutes. A toothpick should come out clean when it is done.

Let cool slightly and enjoy with a glass of Port wine and a nod towards the lovely spirit of Julia!

Three Generations
My mother holding a photograph of her grandparents,
with her father's shadow reflected in the photograph's glass

Index